THE REAL READER'S QUARTERLY

Slightly Foxed

'A World of Shining Beauty'

NO.33   SPRING 2012

Editors Gail Pirkis and Hazel Wood
Marketing and publicity Stephanie Allen and Jennie Paterson
Subscriptions Alarys Gibson, Richard Conyngham and Anna Kirk

Cover illustration: Andy Lovell, 'Creek'
Cover fox: James Nunn, 'Fenland Eel-Trapper'

For the last 20 years Andy Lovell has enjoyed a successful career as an illustrator.
He has also had regular exhibitions of his printmaking, which has now become the main
focus of his work. Drawing and painting from life form the starting-point for his images,
which are then honed, simplified and transformed through silkscreen and monoprint.
For further details see www.andylovell.com.

Design by Octavius Murray

Layout by Andrew Evans

Colophon and tailpiece by David Eccles

© The contributors 2012

Published by Slightly Foxed Limited
67 Dickinson Court
15 Brewhouse Yard
London ECIV 4JX

tel 020 7549 2121/2111
fax 0870 1991245
e-mail all@foxedquarterly.com
www.foxedquarterly.com

Slightly Foxed is published quarterly in early March, June, September and December
Annual subscription rates (4 issues)
UK £36; Europe £44; Rest of the World £48
Concessions are available for those aged 26 or under: please call the office
Single copies of this issue can be bought for £9 (UK), £11 (Europe) or £12 (Rest of the World)
Back issues are also available

ISBN 978-1-906562-35-9

Printed and bound by Smith Settle, Yeadon, West Yorkshire

Contents

Contents

Rosalind Bliss, 'Ducks and Daffodils'

Our bookshop can obtain any of the books mentioned in this issue.
Slightly Foxed on Gloucester Road, 123 Gloucester Road,
London SW7 4TE, e-mail: enquiries@foxedbooks.com, tel: 020 7370 3503

From the Editors

Now the year has turned and spring bulbs are bravely poking up in Clerkenwell window-boxes, we're looking forward hopefully, as well as looking back thoughtfully over the events of the past year, which was quite an adventurous one for *SF*.

The highlight, perhaps, was our first Readers' Day, held in November at the Art Workers' Guild in Bloomsbury. It was a day that more than lived up to expectations. The setting – an elegant Georgian house which has been a home-from-home for craftsmen since the days of William Morris – felt perfect, spacious yet friendly. The day was packed in every sense and we were surprised and touched to learn of the distant places from which many people had travelled to be there, including the Isle of Wight and even the South of France. It was a great pleasure to see so many *Slightly Foxed* readers gathered together – a 'fellowship of readers', as Daisy Hay put it in the introduction to her talk on the early nineteenth-century circle who feature in her book *The Young Romantics* – and names were put to voices which had previously been heard only on the phone. The bookshop which Tony and Jane had set up was humming, and at teatime delicious cakes made by our versatile contributor Frances Donnelly were served. We enjoyed the whole thing hugely and are now planning another Readers' Day this coming November.

In the autumn we also launched the first title in our new paperback series – Ysenda Maxtone Graham's *Mr Tibbits's Catholic School*. We'd been thinking for some time of putting into paperback those Slightly Foxed Editions that have now sold out, and when the hardback of *Mr Tibbits* disappeared from the shelves in record time and orders were still pouring in, it seemed the moment to start. Now we have also added Diana Holman-Hunt's *My Grandmothers and I* to the series. Though we say it ourselves, the new paperbacks are delightful – pocket-sized and elegantly produced on the same good cream paper as *SF*. So if you missed these two titles first time round, here's your chance.

Which brings us to the latest of the Slightly Foxed Editions – Suzanne St Albans' magical *Mango and Mimosa*, a recommendation for which appeared in our very first issue, and which we're now able to publish ourselves (see p.11). It's the story of a childhood spent in a most eccentric pre-war household, moving restlessly between an old farmhouse in a remote part of Southern France and the plantation Suzanne's intellectual and pathologically anti-social father had inherited in Malaya. Hers is an entirely individual voice and her story is filled with unforgettable characters, both human and animal. Truly one of the funniest and most atmospheric memoirs we've read.

Another individual voice is that of the novelist John Cowper Powys, and on p.33 the philosopher and critic John Gray shares his enthusiasm for the work of that largely forgotten writer. This will form the basis of a talk he'll be giving at 4 p.m. in the Library at Christ Church on Saturday, 24 March, as part of the Oxford Literary Festival. For any of you who would like to attend, or indeed enjoy a longer visit to the Festival, there will be a discount for *SF* readers on tickets for the event and accommodation can be reserved in college. For details please call the *Slightly Foxed* office.

And finally, the winner of our Christmas crossword competition (the answers to which appear on p.94) is Sir John Sparrow, who receives a year's free subscription to *Slightly Foxed*. We send him our congratulations, and wish you all happy reading this year.

GAIL PIRKIS

HAZEL WOOD

A World of Shining Beauty

GEE WILLIAMS

My small Welsh primary school lay at the end of Boundary Lane, on the Flintshire-Cheshire border. It was a good 20 miles from any beach. Nevertheless, the first thing I remember having to learn was 'Sea Fever', possibly the best-known poem at that time in the English-speaking world.

This was the Sixties and 'I must go down to the seas again, to the lonely sea and the sky' had been taken to heart by successive generations before mine. The entire class would soon be word-perfect with 'And all I ask is a merry yarn from a laughing fellow-rover, /And quiet sleep and a sweet dream when the long trick's over.' I suspect most of us had only a vague idea of the poem's meaning. Next Miss Roberts made an attempt on 'Cargoes', but the 'Dirty British coaster with a salt-caked smoke stack' defeated us.

Written when their author was only 24, both poems are by John Masefield. Born into a modest Herefordshire home in 1878, at his death in 1967 he was Poet Laureate, Doctor of Letters, novelist, playwright, critic and a literary lion on both sides of the Atlantic. The response now to mention of him is usually dismissive but for me two lines from those lessons stuck fast, though neither 'Sea Fever' nor 'Cargoes' furnished them. They were: 'One road leads to London, /One road leads to Wales.' As an adolescent I misread them, thinking they were a celebration of 'getting out there'. But they made me curious enough to read as an adult *Grace before Ploughing*, which Masefield describes as 'Fragments of Autobiography'.

John Masefield, *Grace before Ploughing* (1966), is out of print.

Motherless at 6, by 12 every adult with an interest in the young John Masefield was either dead or, in his father's case, committed to an asylum. Foisted on an aunt, he was denied access to the books that were his solace and sent to toughen up as a cadet at HMS *Conway*. (Not resentful, he would one day write its history.) At 16, on his first voyage, aboard the four-master barque *Gilcruix*, he rounded the Horn but was stricken by sickness and then by sunstroke and had to be invalided home. A cold reception from the aunt goaded him into trying again. When he reached New York he jumped ship, preferring life as a hobo to more of 'the wheel's kick and the wind's song and the white sail's shaking'. Eventually he got a job in a carpet factory in Yonkers and in his spare time resumed the programme of self-education begun at HMS *Conway*. He read widely, buying 20 books a week, but it was Chaucer who opened his eyes to poetry. In 1897 he returned to England and began to write, his poems reflecting his experience at sea of nature's lethal beauty pitted against human grit. 'Sea Fever', 'Cargoes' and the like were born out of that.

The extraordinary thing is that none of this appears in Masefield's 'autobiography'. When he sat down to write it in the mid-1960s, he knew he was approaching the time 'when the long trick's over'. *Grace before Ploughing* is no misery memoir, but his last word on the beloved Herefordshire border country he was forced to leave. In these glittering fragments he retrieves his impressions of his first six years and eight months when he 'lived in Paradise'. The impressions come, he claims, 'from a memory that has forgotten much, but what memory exists is vivid beyond all other memories'.

We can discount the disclaimer. His recall is superb and where gaps occur it is because, as he admits in exasperation, he didn't go and look *when he had the chance*. The teams of mummers at Ledbury's October Fair are a good example. 'I grieve that I never saw these!' So Masefield torments himself with missing the last performers of the old, lost plays, preferring, as any child would, the cheapjacks and the merry-go-rounds. As for the rest, his descriptions are precise in every line, shaded so cleverly that the whole ninety pages work on you like a painting by Seurat. The dabs of colour are pretty enough – but stand back and there lies an entire landscape.

And what a landscape: the scene is conventionally ravishing, but it is filtered through Masefield's immature mind to produce something not adult or childish but fantastical. A brighter bright is suddenly shot through with black lightning: on his favourite waterway, to attain 'a lovely reach' for swimming or fishing, he must pass 'a very terrible . . . drowning place for unwanted dogs'. The book proceeds in a series of individual episodes: a chapter on the subject of terrors is followed by one on moles and moleskin. Another on the Romans softens you up for prize-fights but fails to prepare you for the killing of a stag.

Peter Reddick

In the year the Harrier jump jet made its maiden flight and the Rolling Stones played at the Hollywood Bowl, Masefield was writing from personal recollection. More than once I was forced to flick back and check on that 'First published 1966'.

Each episode whets the appetite for the next so that ninety pages fly by without your noticing the extraordinary omissions. There is hardly a reference to family or to any named friend. Instead Masefield takes refuge in the passive voice: 'Here I was helped to get down, and was shown how I was to go alone on the hill, just below the first great trench, and watch them coming to me by the usual path to the summit. It was my first free walk on any Malvern hill . . .' The rest of the party – *them* – were soon to be snatched away. And before many more years that little figure seen stoutly labouring up the 'rough wild hill' would be ejected from a Paradise he knew 'better than the grown-up knows his parish'.

Once out there Masefield did 'make it', through extraordinary effort. There was early success with his *Salt-Water Ballads*, from which legions of rote-learners, myself included, can still quote. In 1923 his *Collected Poems* sold 80,000 copies. Yet Masefield the man remained diffident. (As Poet Laureate he submitted new work to *The Times* and always included a stamped addressed envelope in case of rejection.)

Sadly 'Sea Fever' and 'Cargoes' and the long narrative poems that followed have failed to find a new audience. Unlike Housman, Masefield is unfashionably straight. If exotic, he somehow lacks Kipling's glamour. Despite individual lyrics of rare intensity he has become what marketing men would call 'a big ask'. Of his prose, *The Midnight Folk* and *The Box of Delights*, written for children, are in print, reinvented by Quentin Blake's quirky illustrations. *The Bird of Dawning*, the rollicking young man's adventure that appealed to me most as a teenager (I was odd), is available courtesy of the National Maritime Museum. To read his 'Fragments of Autobiography', though, you will have to scour the second-hand bookshops.

A long and happy marriage to a loving older woman, two children and an embarrassment of honours were to come to the boy of *Grace before Ploughing*. So often the deviser of anthems for other men's lives, Masefield ends it with a pure, fresh image for his own: 'the scramble up in a world of shining beauty . . . seeing all manner of strangeness'.

GEE WILLIAMS is afflicted with a borderer's chronic failure to settle, being a poet, playwright, broadcaster, novelist and short-story writer.

All Creatures Great and Small

HAZEL WOOD

In the early days of *Slightly Foxed*, in our very first issue in fact, I wrote about a book that had once come my way in the course of my work as a publisher's editor – a book that had entranced me. Suzanne St Albans' memoir *Mango and Mimosa* told the story of her eccentric upbringing in the 1920s and '30s, when her family moved restlessly between the home her two lovable but ill-assorted parents had created out of the ruins of an old farmhouse near Vence, at the foot of the Alpes-Maritimes, and Assam Java, the plantation her father had inherited in Malaya, at Selangor.

I wrote this piece long before our Slightly Foxed Editions were even thought of, and as with a number of other memoirs we featured in our early issues, which have now slipped out of print, we're delighted to be able to reissue this lovable book as the latest SFE. So, for those readers who haven't already made its acquaintance, this is a brief introduction, and a reminder for those who have.

Reading it again has made me think about what makes a successful memoir. Primarily, I suppose, it is the writer's ability to speak to the reader with an entirely individual voice, and that is certainly true of Suzanne St Albans (or Suzanne Fesq, as she was until she married the 13th Duke of St Albans in 1947 – an event too far in the future to feature here). From the opening page one has the sense of being with someone funny and spontaneous, with tremendous zest and an original take on life, and an acute and affectionate eye for the oddities of human – and animal – behaviour.

She also has a wonderful ability to evoke the feeling of those places where she spent her childhood – the dreamy atmosphere of the old

Provençal farmhouse, which her parents christened Mas Mistral – 'after the poet, not the wind' – along the front of which 'ran a balcony festooned with bignonia, wisteria and moonflowers climbing up from the terrace below, so that for six months of the year at least the whole front was covered with thick clusters of flowers'. And the steamy jungle heat of Assam Java, where electric storms thundered around the sky, and where the children were never allowed to run on the upper floor of the house lest it collapse, because the timbers were riddled with termites: 'We slept under the rafters and the palm leaf roof . . . Rats and squirrels peered down at us, snakes and insects of every kind crawled in and out of the palm thatch, and frequently plumped to the floor with a thud and a squelch.'

In fact living creatures of all kinds featured large in the Fesq household, for Marie, their father's severe Swiss nanny who had been pressed into service again when he himself produced children, was a keen naturalist. The nursery shelves were filled with bottles of pickled specimens, and in the courtyard at Assam Java lived a menagerie of assorted creatures, some rescued, some adopted, with broken legs or wings expertly mended by Marie. Baby birds fallen from the nest were fed mashed-up worms with stamp-collecting tweezers, the little household monkey curled up on any convenient lap, a rescued stork liked to join the family at badminton, and Titi the pet hen, assisted by a small ladder, laid her eggs in the nursery wardrobe among the children's clothes.

Marie, morbid and disciplinarian though she might have been, was the fixed point in the children's turning world, and they adored her. She in turn adored their father and disliked (and no doubt envied) their mother – he a frail and intellectual recluse, who found family life a dreadful strain and hid in the cellar when visitors came, she a sociable, restless, impulsive being, who Marie felt was frivolous and a bad influence generally. Madame Fesq's attitude to education was certainly casual to say the least, and Suzanne was pulled in and out of establishments ranging from the local village school in Provence to a grim convent in Paris and a girls' school in Littlehampton – none of which lasted long.

Another fixed point for Suzanne, her brother and two sisters were the idyllic summers the family spent on the long white beaches of the Atlantic coast, where they met up with their mother's friends the Darlanges. From the beginning the Darlanges' handsome son Jacques was Suzanne's bosom pal. As they both grew up, he clearly began to want a different, more adult relationship, but, tomboy that she still was, she wasn't ready, and shied away. It's a wonderful account of the confusions, embarrassments and misunderstandings of first love.

Then in the late summer of 1939 war was declared. The German Occupation scattered the two families to the winds, with the Fesqs – who for complicated reasons had British passports – fleeing to England and forced to abandon Marie in France. Meantime their father was marooned in South-east Asia, where he spent most of the war in a prison camp. It was the end of Suzanne's childhood, and the point at which this story ends.

I met the late Duchess briefly only once, when she was in her eighties, but I learned from her obituaries that during the war she had worked in Psychological Warfare as a news writer in North Africa and Italy, and then in 1945 in Austria where she met and fell in love with the amusing and dashing Colonel Charles Beauclerk. When he finally inherited the dukedom (at birth he was only ninth in line), it came with a string of titles, including that of Grand Falconer of England, but very little else. In an effort to recoup the family fortunes he embarked on an ill-advised business career which foundered spectacularly and ignominiously in 1973, and they lost virtually everything.

So he and the Duchess retired to Mas Mistral where, in her usual spirited way, she took up her pen and produced this memoir – partly, presumably, in the hope of making some money, and partly perhaps to recapture some of that happy lost childhood world – as well, apparently, as 'five other non-fiction books' which I have been unable to trace. Not bad for someone whose first language was French, and who never seems to have gone to school for more than a year at a time – though perhaps that was her saving grace, for she retained a youthful enthusiasm and freshness which permeate this funny and magical memoir. She was certainly quite a gal.

HAZEL WOOD grew up with a menagerie of creatures, but is now petless following the sudden tragic death of Dan the cat.

Suzanne St Albans' *Mango and Mimosa* (256pp), is now available from *Slightly Foxed* in a new limited and numbered cloth-bound pocket edition of 2,000 copies, each priced at £12.50 (plus p&p: UK £2.50, Europe £4.50, Rest of the World £5.50). Copies may be ordered by post (67 Dickinson Court, 15 Brewhouse Yard, London EC1V 4JX), by phone (020 7549 2121) or via our website www.foxedquarterly.com.

In Praise of Pratchett

AMANDA THEUNISSEN

OF COURSE, SINCE YOU BELIEVE IN REINCAR-NATION said Death to Bjorn Hammerlock [the recently murdered dwarf in Terry Pratchett's *Men at Arms*], YOU WILL BE BJORN AGAIN.

He waited.

WAS THERE ANYTHING AMUSING IN THE STATE-MENT I JUST MADE? IT WAS A PUNE OR PLAY ON WORDS. I'VE BEEN TOLD I SHOULD TRY AND MAKE THE OCCASION A LITTLE MORE ENJOYABLE.

'Bjorn again?'

YES.

'I'll think about it.'

THANK YOU.

Death turns up a lot in Terry Pratchett's books. He's one of his most popular characters, a seven-foot-high skeleton with burning blue eyes who speaks in CAPITALS. He is as terrifying as one would expect – except that he has a real horse called Binky (the skeleton ones kept falling apart), loves curry, can't play chess and has a deep compassion for all the living things whose lives he terminates. I find it a curiously comforting image.

Death personifies for Pratchett a lot of the themes he thinks are important: the strangeness of the universe and Man's place in it; the

Terry Pratchett, *Small Gods* (Discworld Novel 13) (1992)
Corgi · Pb · 390pp · £7.99 · ISBN 9780552152976

human capacity for self-deception; the fact that few things are exactly as they seem and that it is vital to think for yourself.

It's no secret that Pratchett himself has early-onset Alzheimer's. For a man of his devotion to words, sparkling wit, breadth of erudition and memory, it seems particularly cruel. He has already donated $1 million to research, but as his recent television documentary showed, he is also a fervent proponent of assisted suicide. 'My life, my death, my choice,' he says. It's not an issue that has yet been covered in his books, but maybe it's only a matter of time. However, it is not his courage and wisdom in life I want to praise, but those qualities in his work.

Pratchett writes fantasy novels. Many people whose judgement I respect just don't get him, finding the plots ludicrous and the humour childish. Many more are possibly put off by the lurid covers, heaving with dwarves, dragons, vampires, goblins, trolls, and busty blondes bursting from their tightly fitting armour. But there are also those, like me, who discovered his books early, read them all, like most of them and devour each new one with greedy pleasure. I must confess to having once covered the newest with brown paper and labelled it *The Principles of Geology* in an attempt to disguise it from my clamouring family.

What I would like to do is persuade the reluctant to pick up just one and give him a chance.

There are 39 adult Discworld novels, 13 for children and young adults, and endless adaptations for stage and television, compendiums, science books, graphic books and even a cookery book. They run in rough chronological order but each stands alone.

The Discworld is a small, flat world supported by four enormous elephants standing on the turtle Great A'Tuin, which swims slowly through space. It's basically a medieval world where magic is the norm. Pratchett has said he focuses on fantasy because 'It's easier to bend the universe around the story and it isn't just about wizards and silly wands. It's about seeing the world from new directions.' Within this world, humans, witches, wizards, trolls, dwarves, vampires and various forms of the undead live recognizably human lives. Dwarves and trolls abandon the hard life of mines and mountains for the big city of Ankh-Morpork, where they work in shops or act as hit-men and generally try to make better lives for their children. Golems, gnomes and zombies join the police force where Sergeant Angua, a werewolf, is already extremely successful in both her shapes. The difficulty of running a multi-species police force and trying to be honest in a dishonest world drives many of the books.

The context is crucial. Unlike *Dr Who*, which has accustomed us to strange races inhabiting the universe, the Discworld doesn't really work on television. I think this is because the contrast between the essentially normal behaviour of the inhabitants and the upside-downness of Discworld is lost on screen. And a lot of the jokes don't work because they are too literary and too clever.

Pratchett published his first short story when he was 15 and he has been writing ever since. I find the early books, which are parodies of science fiction, fun but not memorable. Then in 1990 came *Moving Pictures*, the first to introduce real-world modern innovations into this fantasy medieval setting. It's about film-making and is stuffed with references to early Hollywood. The hero has a thin moustache, 'can't sing, can't dance, can handle a sword a little' and stars in a ten-minute three-reeler epic about the Civil War called *Blown Away*. The book's about the magic of movies and the power of dreams, for good and evil, and the need to grab life's chances as and when you can.

It was followed by a string of other books with a serious idea at the heart of the jokes – journalism and the power of print (*The Truth*); rock and roll (*Soul Music*); the Gulf War (*Jingo*); feminism (*The Monstrous Regiment*); Egyptian history (*Pyramids*); and high finance (*Making Money*). Astronomy, university politics, science, sport and trades unions all appear. And the underlying philosophy is consistent. Pratchett is a staunch republican, against organized religion, anti-authoritarian whether it's priests or politicians, anti-racist and a firm supporter of women. He has several strong heroines including

Granny Weatherwax, the doyenne of witches, and serious, practical Susan, Death's adopted granddaughter, who occasionally and reluctantly takes over Death's duties for him.

Pratchett says that to write, you must read to overflowing on every subject. He cites P. G. Wodehouse, Jerome K. Jerome, G. K. Chesterton and Mark Twain as influences and has clearly obeyed his own rule and read incredibly widely. The combination of anachronism and strong stories gives his books their richly distinctive style, with references to religion, anthropology, philosophy, natural history, politics, science, music, literature and history all in the mix. In fact, working out the references is half the fun.

Like this, from *Wyrd Sisters* (basically *Macbeth* with real witches). Hwel, the dwarf playwright whose head is full of ideas whose time has not yet come, is having trouble with his new play.

> He'd sorted out the falling chandelier and found a place for a villain who wore a mask to conceal his disfigurement and rewritten one of the funny bits to allow for the fact that the hero had been born in a handbag. It was the clowns that were giving him trouble again . . . one fat and one thin – 'thys ys a main Dainty Messe you have got me into, Stanleigh . . .' He had laughed until his chest ached and the rest of the company had looked on in astonishment. But in his dreams it was hilarious.

One critic has described his style as philosophical badinage interspersed with slapstick. What Pratchett loves is words and the way they can be turned and twisted. The jokes are thrown away with mad generosity and, as always with humour, it's hard to pull examples off the page – you have to be there! One joke in *Truckers*, a children's book, is a good example. Trying to escape the planet, small alien Nomes are driving a stolen lorry and see a sign coming up.

> 'Looks like "Road Works Ahead",' said Grimma in a puzzled voice.

'Yes but', said Masklin, 'why say it? I mean, you could understand "Road Doesn't Work Ahead" – why tell us it works?'

'Sometimes', said Gemma, 'I think humans really don't understand anything about the proper use of language.'

Daniel Macklin

There are so many Discworld books it's easy to pick up a less good one and be put off for ever. When I am proselytizing on behalf of Pratchett I suggest *Small Gods* as the best starting-point. This is a satire on institutionalized religion, calcified by form and custom and corrupted by power. It's also about the nature of belief, spiritual regeneration and forgiveness. His theory is that gods need believers and men want gods. There are gods of every size and shape in the Discworld, jostling for space and power in a game of celestial snakes and ladders. Belief is their food without it they slide down the snake and dwindle away to an unheard voice, chittering in the desert. It's a god-eat-god world where only the ones with enough believers survive.

Small Gods is the story of the once-great god Om of Omnia – currently manifested as an elderly tortoise – and the ignorant novice Brutha, his only true believer. It tells how Brutha grows in stature and wisdom to become a true prophet, and how Om acquires a sense of responsibility and compassion, and becomes a true god.

In his time Om was a ferocious Old Testament god, smiting and trampling the heathen, and holding that respect equalled fear and fear equalled belief. 'If the price isn't high,' he asks Brutha, 'how can people respect you?' Looking after his believers or helping them live good lives is not on the agenda. He's trying to make his way back up the ladder but something is missing. Then he reads in an old book by an ancient philosopher: 'Around the Godde there forms a shelle of Prayers and Ceremonies and Buildings and Priests and Authority, until at Last the Godde Dies. And this maye notte be noticed.' And he realizes no one actually believes in gods any more. Except Brutha.

Brutha not only believes in Om, he believes every word Om is ever reported to have said. Om apparently dictated all 193 Precepts to the prophet Ossery from a pillar of flame in the desert. By them, the people of Omnia live – or die painfully. Om remembers the pillar of fire but not Ossory and is even less sure about the Precepts.

'I don't think I did that,' said Om doubtfully. 'I'm sure I would have remembered 193 chapters.'

'What did you say to him then?'

'As far as I can remember, it was "Hey, see what I can do!"' said the tortoise.

Brutha stared at it. It looked embarrassed, insofar as that's possible for a tortoise.

'Even gods like to relax,' it said.

'But if you've been down here as a tortoise, who has been listening to the prayers? Who has been accepting the sacrifices? Who has been judging the dead?'

'I don't know,' said the tortoise. 'Who did it before?'

'You did!'

'Did I?'

So much for Moses and the Burning Bush.

Small Gods is Pratchett at his best – erudite, subversive and very funny – and the best place to start. After that, you're on your own. And if you still can't bring yourself to pick up a luridly coloured paperback, there is a scholarly edition of *Small Gods*. Plain black cover, sober lettering, no monsters. Everyone will think you're reading a serious study of comparative religion – which in many ways you are. Just give it a try.

AMANDA THEUNISSEN is a journalist and television producer who tries to follow Terry Pratchett's rule and reads to overflowing.

Teaching Life

GRANT MCINTYRE

Richard Cobb was a history don at Balliol, eccentric in a college where oddness is almost routine. He was small and thin, not very prepossessing. Jeremy Lewis, his editor at Chatto & Windus, described him as 'like a freshly skinned rabbit, red and blue all over and faintly clammy to the touch'. He was certainly memorable to those he taught; Tim Hilton remembered an 'utter disregard for decorum and discipline. I still hear the French martial music and the crashing of glasses. He was both an example of the scholarly life and a lord of misrule.' Out of college he was memorable too: Lewis wrote of walking with him after a lunch where as always he'd had plenty to drink. 'Suddenly, ramrod stiff and with no bending of the knees, Cobb toppled over backwards. His head was only inches from the pavement when I caught him, like Nureyev catching Fonteyn . . .' Alcohol and anarchy were always magnets. There was no gathering so distinguished he'd avoid being thrown out of it.

Naturally there was more to him than this. A fellow historian said Cobb had a poet's imagination. He started his academic life by tunnelling into archives throughout France, not attached to any university, pursuing his own interest in the Revolution, or rather in

---

Richard Cobb, *The French and Their Revolution: Selected Writings* and *Paris and Elsewhere: Selected Writings* (both edited by David Gilmour, 1998) are out of print, as are his English memoirs, *Still Life: Sketches from a Tunbridge Wells Childhood* (1983), *A Classical Education* (1985), *Something to Hold Onto: Autobiographical Sketches* (1988) and *The End of the Line: A Memoir* (1997).

the people caught up in it. Some of these people really were committed to *Liberté* etc. but, for most, revolution meant dodging the
dangerous busybodies of the new order, or a chance to dump res-
ponsibilities, or an opportunity for crime. Cobb followed whatever
unexpected path took his eye – the love letters of a *guillotiné*, inter-
cepted correspondence from London or eye-witness accounts of a
massacre – and became addicted to France's various collections and
bibliothèques, most never consulted from one century's end to the
next. Those early years, solitary but for the dead, honed his compassion and were a source of his originality.

There were other disparities in his make-up, for instance the different selves he inhabited on either side of the Channel: 'I do not say
the same things in French as I do in English, because I am not the
same person.' And though he liked the distinctions that came his
way – Professor, CBE, FBA, *chevalier de la Légion d'honneur* – he
was more at home in dubious bars and mean streets in Paris or Lyon.
A particular friend, Maurice Chauvirey, was a burglar and black-
marketeer who celebrated the Liberation of France by liberating a
German army truck and using it to liberate the contents of French
farmhouses whose owners had not yet returned.

His nature was full of such splits, but for him there was no split
between history and experience. He brought to them both the same
empathy and understood in the same way the needs and sometimes
sordid shifts of individual lives. David Gilmour said 'he wrote with
such intuition about the poor of revolutionary France because he
knew their descendants in the 1940s and '50s: having spent so much
time with peasant farmers, black-marketeers, criminals, legionnaires,
sailors and their families, he was naturally more aware than most historians of their feelings and preoccupations . . . His revolutionary
armies did not, therefore, consist simply of revolutionary enthusiasts
but also of people who joined up because they liked uniforms,
because they were unemployed or bankrupt, or because they were
returning émigrés or counter-revolutionaries in need of a disguise.'

Cobb was only interested in lives and relationships. He dismissed theories of history that tried to impose structure on human chaos. Methodology was the invention of solemn Germans. In the same way, he recoiled from all political ideology; in fact he distrusted authority throughout his life. When a fellow don called him an anarchist he famously took it as a compliment.

Richard Cobb by Deborah Elliott,
1984. National Portrait Gallery

*

Cobb knew more about the Revolution than anyone, French or otherwise. He was not the first Englishman to write about it but he was certainly a pioneer in actually going to France to look at evidence close up. He was not much interested in Louis XVI, Marie Antoinette, or Danton, Marat or the others, though he did like to spot Robespierres in modern life. He hadn't much to say about the Tennis Court Oath or the Fall of the Bastille, and that is really a relief since for most of us the Revolution's politics is a mass of forgettable detail. To enjoy Cobb's evocation of life in its midst, you need only the following oversimplified summary: (1) the attempt to replace government by aristos with something less grasping; (2) the rage of those who wanted speedier and ideally more brutal results; (3) the Republic of Virtue, which was actually a bloodbath; (4) the chaotic retaliation; (5) Napoleon.

Having no time for theories, Cobb had none for anatomies of revolution either. He claimed not to know what had set the French one off, since the discontents were hardly new. Each revolution is unique and unprecedented, he said, otherwise it would easily be headed off by the forces of law and order. The flash that creates the explosion is hard to contrive, or explain, and so it was in 1789. Frustration, resentment, boredom, failure were all vital. But once the fire was lit, the usual people appeared: discontented lawyers for the Committees, *sans-culottes* to be the shock troops on the street. These latter included plenty of opportunists and score-settlers, and generally the sharp-elbowed coped as they always do. But the Revolution was never, Cobb said, for the *many*. 'It had nothing to offer the vast body of the poor, of vagrants, beggars, the sick, the old, the cold, abandoned children . . . save worse conditions [and] better repression.'

It was characteristic of Cobb that he would combine the extremes of human experience with the minutiae. He had an eye for revealing trivia and was attuned to language. The more aggressive revolutionaries went in for the cannibalistic, always threatening to eat each other's livers or proposing a fry-up of aristocrat. On the other hand revolutionary babies, when saints' names had fallen from grace, might be given more vegetarian names, such as Haricot, Endive or even Absinthe. As with verbal metaphors, so with visual ones. Kings and queens disappeared from revolutionary packs of cards. *Sans-culottes* dispensed with breeches, by definition, but there was also the question of facial hair. Opinion was divided as to whether a moustache was or was not a badge of correctness, though there was no doubt that a beard was a *marque du fanatisme*.

*

Because Cobb's kind of history was so closely engaged with experience, it had to be walked, smelt and drunk, overheard in cafés and railway stations. His studies of the eighteenth century progressed hand-in-hand with his memoirs of the twentieth. He first went to Paris in 1935, when he was 17, and stayed with a well-to-do widow, Mme Thullier. Her two raffish sons went in for horseplay of various kinds, 'attempting to race the Blue Train on the stretch through Villeneuve-Saint-Georges in their mother's enormous black Panhard-Levassor, throwing fish and silver salver over the balcony on Fridays to express their anti-clericalism, driving straight at traffic policemen'. The elder son, François, became an auctioneer. In that role he would 'make a very rapid and businesslike entry on his rostrum, plunging straight into the sale, with a semi-serious description of some grotesque object held up before him, as if it had been a heraldic symbol'. In a single session 'the *bicornes* of *polytechniciens* would be disposed of in company with the shakos of *cyrards* [cadet officers] . . . immense quantities of female clothing, down to the intimacies of night-wear, knickers, shifts, *soutiens-gorges*, would appear on the anatomical shelves in front of his rostrum, as if this had been an unofficial *morgue*, minus the bodies'. Cobb thought François Thullier 'a committed artist, a poet, even a social historian of a kind . . . His curiosity about people was insatiable.'

For Cobb too, people's clothes and belongings revealed their states of mind. His book *Death in Paris* (1978) deals with accidents, murder and – mostly – suicide in the six years from 1795. Many of these deaths happened in the Seine, and from the records of bodies fished out Cobb constructed a picture of life on the lowest rung. The drowned would be identified by their clothes: poor people would 'carry very little with them through life, and most of that *on* them, day and night . . . men who wore two or three pairs of trousers and several waistcoats, did so, not so much to keep warm as in an effort to preserve . . . their wherewithal'. Some even dressed up for their departure, like a highwayman for his hanging.

*

Cobb was aware of terrain in a way most historians are not; he made one see it and feel its importance. Rivers for instance were part of every life. Not all deaths in the Seine were suicides – after all, the river offered poor people their best chance of a bath, and there would be accidents. There were more river-based trades then too, like the millers, or the *flotteurs* who steered the *trains de bois* down fast-flowing rivers to the wood ports of Paris. Then there were the river boats, the cheapest form of transport. They were good for travel, trade and escape, and sometimes also for 'disposal of compromising objects, including unwanted wives or mistresses'. Rivers were the network along which news and rumour spread, and they dictated the pace at which uprisings would travel; Rouen would riot two days after Paris because that was the time the boat took to get the news, the grievance and the enthusiasts that far downstream.

As ever-present as the rivers, and even more alarming, was the sense of being under siege by surrounding wildlife, some of it human. Paris was ringed by 'clusters of turbulent carters' inns, of hutments, of cardboard dwellings and even tents, in which an uncharted, moving population . . . camped, like the Turks outside Vienna'. It was risky to go anywhere near these places. Next to them the forests began. The highroads through those were 'uncertain, fragile frontiers, between huge areas of primeval jungle'. The woods were royal hunting grounds made national property. They quickly became a national firewood supply but there was still plenty of cover for robbery, murder and rape.

In his own life, too, Cobb was sensitive to place. He loved disregarded quarters, with their 'obscure corners, deep courtyards, private *voies sans issue* . . . high front steps leading to street doors that have not been opened for a hundred years . . . the swing doors of a tiny hotel, rue de la Goutte-d'Or, full of menace, evocative of sordid violence'.

*

In his work, Cobb felt a chivalrous concern for women's vulnerability to violence and for the fate of servant girls made pregnant by employers and then fired. He regretted the Revolution's indifference to love, sex and children. In his own life, he had a soft spot for prostitutes and as a young man was on excellent terms with many. He was not at first a good chooser of wives. He was briefly married to an employee of the SNCF whose cheap rail tickets helped him in his research. Later he married a colonel's daughter, a move he afterwards found baffling, as she did too. That was brief as well. There might have been a third marriage when during the Cold War a Bulgarian siren fell for him at some academic conference. But she was warned off by her minders. This episode reads like a story by John le Carré, with the central role played by Monsieur Hulot. Cobb was lucky in the end to marry one of his students, Margaret Tennant, who looked after him patiently till the end of his life.

When he became Professor, Cobb moved from Balliol to Worcester. He loved and despised both colleges. Balliol was full of bleeding hearts, Etonian new leftists and zealous, indefatigable reformers. Several dons were mad and the Master was devious. The Worcester dons on the whole did not bleed – but then 'most of them did not seem to have any blood'. He upset colleagues in both places with his visceral anti-authoritarianism, oddly mixed with admiration for people like Pinochet. But he was much more affable with students; surprisingly, he approved of the toffish end of undergraduate life as much as the French underclass.

In the end, he retired from Oxford and moved with his wife Margaret to Whitby. He was supposed to be writing a new book for John Murray, where I was working at the time. It was to be on the events of Thermidor, the turning-point when the Terror became Counter-Terror. *Thermidor* became one of those books kept in the programme only by unrealistic hope. But Whitby proved isolated and unsatisfactory, and it was abandoned for Abingdon. There in 1996 he died.

Even though *Thermidor* had never been written, we did have in train a final volume of memoirs, to be called *The End of the Line*. That had been delivered as his memoirs always were, typed on pale blue Basildon Bond writing-paper of the smallest size, and handed over to Richard Brain, the wizard who would turn it into a book. Margaret wondered whether we should add to it a piece on his last days, and to that end she and I spent an afternoon in Port Meadow, sitting on the banks of the Isis with an ancient borrowed tape-recorder. It gave us a good deal of trouble. As I sat on the damp grass transfixed by the awful indignities of his illness, and then his horrifying struggle with death itself, I couldn't help thinking that Cobb himself might have appreciated both the occasion and the superannuated tape-recorder, which looked ready to be knocked down for a few francs by his friend François Thullier. But the piece when I wrote it up was too dark even for the last book by the man once called the Goya of historians, and we decided to leave it out.

Where to start reading Cobb? I'd suggest David Gilmour's masterly collections, *The French and Their Revolution* and *Paris and Elsewhere*. He does not, of course, include Cobb's English memoirs, which number among them *Still Life*, a portrait of Tunbridge Wells at the height of its oddity between the wars, and *A Classical Education*, which covers his close but uneasy friendship with a schoolmate convicted of murdering his own mother with an axe.

His students used to claim that only over a long, argumentative and drunken acquaintanceship could the full Cobb personality be felt. In an obituary Philip Mansel remembered him as tutor. 'He did not simply describe, he transformed himself into, a farmer overeating merely for the pleasure of depriving Parisians of their food; [or] a revolutionary who had marinated in envy all his life and was using his position on the Committee of Public Safety for revenge . . . To be taught by Cobb was to be taught life.' Sadly he is no longer around to teach life, but reading him is the next best thing.

GRANT MCINTYRE was once a publisher and is now a sculptor, so he has largely abandoned words and embraced shapes.

How Did He Do It?

RANJIT BOLT

I came to them, the second time, quite late,
It was the day
The letters, full of snobbery and race hate
That caused the chattering classes such dismay
Came out, and Terry Eagleton had pounced:
'Larkin is now beyond the pale,' he'd said,
'All decent folk should chuck him off the shelf.'
As soon as this stiff sentence was pronounced,
Feeling perverse, I picked him up instead
Although (because?) I was a 'wog' myself.

At once I found it didn't matter that
The letters stank:
The skill that, first time round, I'd wondered at,
There it still was, like money in the bank;
The voice did not sound any less humane
As, standing for all human solitude,
He mused on Mr Bleaney in his room;
Nor did I feel less poignantly his pain
When, in the end, he couldn't quite be rude
To wretched Warlock-Williams, by whom

Philip Larkin, *Collected Poems* (2003) · Ed. Anthony Thwaite
Faber · Pb · 192pp · £12.99 · ISBN 9780571216543

Philip Larkin, *Selected Letters* (1993) · Ed. Anthony Thwaite, is out of print.

All social torment was personified –
So sad, and funny;
Or 'Toads' console me less about how I'd
Quite failed to get the 'fame and girl and money'
Even at *sixty* sittings, much less one.
And when I wake in an angst-ridden state
At four a.m., and lie there till the birds
Start singing, and the early, sickening sun
Seeps in, if I should then articulate
My fears, 'Aubade' may well supply the words.

Reading 'The Whitsun Weddings', one's first thought
Is: how's it done?
The prosody's so uniformly taut,
Such deftness is deployed while showing none.
A gentle sadness permeates each line:
Against the couples' happiness we feel
Larkin's own loneliness at having taken
The bachelor path (a life less anodyne,
More painful), hear the humane voice that he'll
Adopt to save his misanthropic bacon.

In 'Dockery and Son' he seems to wear
His solitude
More proudly, though of course the gloom's still there
In fact he's in his blackest ever mood.
Learning that one of his contemporaries
At Oxford is now married with a son
Larkin considers how this came about:
He's single, sonless, while life's Dockeries
Of whom it's mere chance that he isn't one
Blindly and blithely fling their seed about.

'Life is first boredom – then fear',
The tone's as bleak
As even Larkin ever gets. We hear
The voice of existential sorrow speak,
Depressed to madness, nearly, and yet sane.
The 'awful pie' he eats at Sheffield stands
For life itself: such is his eerie knack
With symbols, something utterly mundane
Becomes a powerful image in his hands.
Likewise the gas fire breathing at his back

And the trees swaying, as he starts to write
The note to say
Why, full of anti-social rage and spite,
He can't make drinks in 'Vers de Société'.
The trees and gas fire figure loneliness
Quietly urging Larkin to accept
As he at last, inevitably, does.
These poems' plain tone doesn't make them less
Poetic: symbolism's somehow crept
In the back door, almost eluding us.

Thus windows, in 'High Windows', stand for peace,
A toad for work
In 'Toads'. Significance seems to increase
The duller something is, more meanings lurk.
In the same vein, in 'Church Going', the tone
Is mainly quite colloquial and flat –
'Some brass and stuff up at the holy end' –
The details have a drabness all their own –
The Irish sixpence, cycle-clips and hat
But handling themes – God, Time – that still transcend.

He takes the biggest subjects on alright
But all aimed not
At 'intellectuals' (whom he thought a blight)
But folk in Surbiton, or Aldershot
Like someone in the pub who talks in rhyme –
Always accessible, even when profound,
Wise, unaffected, and 'a decent chap'.
There lies his genius: mixing the sublime
And commonplace: Life, Death, Love, Sex – he'll sound
Them all, and to the depths, but cut the crap.

If he's a flaw, perhaps it's too much gloom
Who likes a snurge?
His poems give his melancholy room
To breathe, and spread itself, but does it purge?
Everyone likes a catchy ditty though
And like so many poets, Larkin's name
Relies, or most, on such: 'This Be the Verse',
'Annus Mirabilis' – it seems these two
(That's not to say he hasn't written worse)
Will always form the bedrock of his fame.

RANJIT BOLT was born in Manchester
In 1959. He spent ten years
In London, working as a stockbroker
Being bored, at first at times, and then to tears
Until he happened upon *Le Menteur*,
A Corneille comedy of some renown
Which hauled him out of limbo, as it were,
Made him the toast (for two ticks) of the town,
Since when he's done enough verse comedies
To drive him, and the public, off their trees.

Every Green Thing

JOHN GRAY

It is hard to know what has made me a lifelong reader of John Cowper Powys, but perhaps the fact that he was one of three very different brothers who shared a common impulse may be part of the explanation. Like many people I read John Cowper first, but it was not long before I fell under the spell of Theodore, whose *Mr Weston's Good Wine* (1927) was still being read when I came across it towards the end of the Sixties. Presented with the lapidary finality one finds in inscriptions in country graveyards, Theodore's allegory tells how Mr Weston and his assistant Michael arrive in the village of Folly Down, selling wine – the light wine that gives pleasure, the heavy dark wine that brings peace – and then vanish into smoke. Reading the book in my late teens I thought it a perfect inversion of conventional religion, showing how a faith that promised eternal life could be reframed as one in which redemption comes in the form of everlasting death.

Some years passed before I immersed myself in Llewelyn, never as widely read a writer. While always acknowledging a saving element of poetry in religion, Llewelyn was a passionate atheist who main-

John Cowper Powys, *Wolf Solent* (1929) · Penguin · Pb · 640pp · £14.99 · ISBN 9780141183992; *A Glastonbury Romance* (1933) · Duckworth · Pb · 1,120pp · £16.99 · ISBN 9780715636480; *Weymouth Sands* (1934) · Duckworth · Pb · 590pp · £12.99 · ISBN 9780715638750; *Maiden Castle* (1936) · Duckworth · Pb · 496pp · £16.99 · ISBN 9780715638910; *Porius* (1951) · Duckworth · Pb · 768pp · £18.95 · ISBN 9780715637326; *Autobiography* (1934) · Faber Finds · Pb · 664pp · £22 · ISBN 9780571271375; *Petrushka and the Dancer*, ed. Morine Krissdottir (1995) · Carcanet · Hb · 352pp · £25 · ISBN 9781857540963.

tained that Christianity had repressed much of the pleasure in life. It was not Llewelyn's polemics against religion that appealed to me – Theodore's parable seemed to me then, as it does today, far more devastating. Rather, it was Llewelyn's vivid stories of how – while suffering from recurrent attacks of the tuberculosis that would eventually kill him – he enjoyed an adventurous career, working as a farmer in Africa, following his brother John to try and make a living as a lecturer in America and travelling to the Middle East and the Caribbean in pursuit of health and interesting sensations. Ever on the brink of life-threatening illness, Llewelyn hated the very idea of death. Yet he managed to turn that fear and revulsion into an exultant embrace of life.

Running through all three writers is the attempt to fashion a practical philosophy that has left behind the hopes embodied in religion. The sons of a man who for more than thirty years was vicar at Montacute in Somerset, each of the brothers had his own distinctive way of leaving the faith of his father. If I like John Cowper best – as most of the time I do – it is because his abiding scepticism about all kinds of belief and disbelief appeals more than Theodore's melancholy paganism or Llewelyn's dogmatic Lucretian certainty. Of course John Cowper was a novelist (and in a small but not insignificant way a poet) rather than a philosopher. But he regarded his writings as propaganda for a particular vision of human life that I find compelling and refreshingly original. Not only the many self-help books he wrote for money – such as his delightful short volume on *The Art of Forgetting the Unpleasant* (1928) – but also his works of fiction were vehicles promoting this distinctive view of things.

The central figures in John Cowper Powys's novels inhabit a landscape that is as much a protagonist in the story as they are themselves. Weymouth is more of a presence in *Weymouth Sands* (1934) than any of the gallery of misfits that makes up the cast of human players. Not the actual Dorset coastal resort that a visitor would have encountered in the Thirties, of course – it is an 'occult Weymouth', Powys tells us at the start of the book, a place distilled from impressions of the place he had accumulated over many years from childhood onwards.

Powys resembles Proust in his intense focus on the central role of sensation and memory in our lives; but unlike Proust the sensations he cherishes most are those that are gathered out of doors. Whereas Proust's world is one of rooms and boulevards, the backdrop against which Powys's characters enact their lives is not a human construction – it is the sky, the sea and the wind. Even Weymouth, which was certainly built by human beings, seems in the novel to have a life of its own that is independent of its architects. As in Hardy's Wessex novels, so in the Wessex novels of John Cowper Powys – *Wolf Solent* (1929), *A Glastonbury Romance* (1933), *Weymouth Sands* and *Maiden Castle* (1936) – an imagined place shapes the lives of the characters regardless of their desires or dreams.

'Chesil Beach in February' by Howard Phipps

In his *Study of Thomas Hardy*, D. H. Lawrence wrote of 'a constant revelation in Hardy's novels: that there exists a great background, vital and vivid, which matters more than the people who move upon it'. Such was Egdon Heath, 'the great self-preservation scheme in which we must all live' and against which any kind of individual self-assertion could only be futile and disastrous. Powys also saw humans as tiny figures moving about in a vast incomprehensible landscape, but for him the upshot was not – as it was for Lawrence – tragedy, but a kind of dogged delight in the world of which humans are such a small part. At times this willed enjoyment rises to the level of an epiphany, as when Powys's *Wolf Solent* watches the sun go down:

> The result of this complete extinction of the sunset was that the world became a world in which every green thing upon its surface received a five-fold addition to its greenness. It was as if an enormous green tidal wave, composed of a substance more translucent than water, had flowed over the whole earth; or rather as if some diaphanous essence of all the greenness created by long days of rain has evaporated during this one moon, only to fall down, with the approach of twilight, in a cold dark emerald-coloured dew.

Finding something of the numinous in the diurnal round, Powys did not despair of the small human world. His response was acceptance, a mix of resolute enjoyment and stoical resignation. It is not by chance that the story of his alter-ego Solent, who finds himself stuck in a web of complex relationships and unfulfilled desires, ends with him having a cup of tea.

The view of things that John Cowper Powys championed could hardly be less fashionable today, for it offers no hope that humans can transform their lives. Instead, Powys has his characters re-envision the world in which they find themselves. What he was describing was a non-religious version of the contemplative life, but for him contemplation was not in the least other-worldly – the search for peace in some realm of the spirit. For him the life of contemplation meant perpetual inner warfare, an incessant struggle to snatch sensations of earthly beauty from the jaws of time. Set in provincial England somewhere between late Victorian times and the interwar years in which they were written, these novels are galleries of brilliant impressions, which have not dated. While the countryside that Powys loved has vanished, the mingling of outward sensation with the inner flux of memory and desire that he portrays in his characters is everyone's experience.

Powys was a dauntingly prolific author, producing not only many minor works but also that vast epic of the Welsh dark ages *Porius* (1951), which I have never been able to finish. He was also one of the twentieth century's great diarists, recording for several decades his everyday impressions and eccentricities. (A selection from the diaries covering some of the most eventful years in Powys's life can be found in *Petrushka and the Dancer. The Diaries of John Cowper Powys, 1929 –1939*, selected and edited by Powys's biographer Morine Krissdottir (1995).) With its unique combination of candour and concealment, Powys's *Autobiography* (1934) must be one of the great confessional memoirs of all time. But for me the core of Powys's work will always be the Wessex novels, since it is in these re-imaginings of the landscape he knew best that his vision of life is most powerfully conveyed.

John Cowper Powys spent much of his life preaching a practical philosophy in which practical life is not very important. A charismatic figure whose lectures electrified audiences across America, he used his position as a sort of secular hedge-priest to try to convert his audiences to a life of sensation. In his *Autobiography* he described himself as a disciple of Pyrrho, the founder of Greek scepticism, and there is some truth in the description. For a sceptic nothing can be known of the nature of things; but the world of the senses remains an undeniable given. Powys did not promote the life of contemplation by marshalling a succession of arguments. He did not believe (any more than I do) that argumentation can change the way people live. Instead he chose to illustrate what such a life might be like, showing fictional figures – often versions of himself – fumbling their way towards acceptance. Along the way he produced some of the most life-enhancing literature in the English language.

JOHN GRAY's most recent book is *The Immortalization Commission: The Strange Quest to Cheat Death*.

Much More than a Perfect Gent

URSULA BUCHAN

I cannot think of many garden writers from a century ago in whose company I would have felt entirely comfortable. William Robinson would have ignored me, Gertrude Jekyll seen through me, and Reginald Farrer unnerved me. But I should dearly have loved to meet Edward Augustus ('Gussie') Bowles, and have him conduct me around his garden one sunny day in spring. For by all accounts he was a sweet-tempered and charming, funny and self-deprecating, discerning and cultured man. He spent his entire life at Myddelton House in Bulls Cross, near Enfield, and, around the beginning of the First World War, wrote what amounted to a gardening autobiography, the trilogy *My Garden in Spring*, *My Garden in Summer* and *My Garden in Autumn and Winter* (1914–15). Of these, the first volume is the best.

Bowles's ancestors, who were Huguenots, had lived at Myddelton House since 1724, and the family owned a majority share in the New River Company, whose eponymous stream flowed through the garden and on to water London. The spacious house (now owned by the Lee Valley Regional Park Authority) is of white Suffolk brick, and was built by Bowles's grandfather in 1818 (he pulled down an Elizabethan red-brick house to do it).

E. A. Bowles's books can sometimes be obtained, at a price, from secondhand book specialists, and there are a number of facsimiles in circulation, in particular a Timber Press edition of *My Garden in Spring* (Pb · 404pp · $24.95 · ISBN 9781604690415). The recently renovated gardens at Myddelton House are open daily, without admission charge: see www.eabowlessociety.org.uk.

Gussie lost most of the use of his right eye as a result of an infection when he was 8, a fact which prevented his being sent to Harrow, like his brothers. Instead, he was taught the classics by a local clergyman, and he developed a keen interest in natural history while ranging around the garden at home. He went up to Cambridge to read Theology and would have taken Holy Orders had the deaths of a brother and sister from tuberculosis not intervened. He abandoned ordination in order to look after his parents, and became a lay reader and churchwarden instead

Bowles's parents were full of Christian charity, doing good works among the poor of Enfield, and their children inherited these philanthropic tendencies. Gussie founded a night school to educate poor boys and organized the local Boys' Brigade. He did not need to seek employment, so settled instead for developing a prodigious interest in gardening at Myddelton House, making it his own after his father died in 1918 and he inherited a life interest in the house. Scarcely anything changed for the rest of his life: the house remained as it had been, with all the Victorian ornaments and furnishings that his mother had liked and without gas, electricity or heating.

Gussie quickly became known as a noted gardener, plantsman and plant-hunter, and also a talented botanical artist, working mainly in watercolours. He was particularly fascinated by flowering bulbs, rock plants, cacti and botanical eccentricities, such as the corkscrew willow and the purple-leaved plantain. He placed these 'curiosities' in a bed together, which he called the Lunatic Asylum. He was, really, in a direct line of descent from those seventeenth-century London botanists John Gerard and John Parkinson. His reputation grew steadily and, in 1900, he was asked to sit on the Scientific Committee of the Royal Horticultural Society, something he continued to do until a month before his death in 1954, aged 89.

In the trilogy, Bowles adopted the literary device of conducting the reader around the 6-acre garden at Myddelton House, border by border, cold frame by cold frame. Sound practical advice and closely observed botanical information were intertwined with gently amusing anecdotes and lyrical descriptions. His discursive style was criticized in a review in the *Times Literary Supplement*, after *My Garden in Spring* was published, but personally I find him hard to beat. How about this as a brilliant and useful explanation of how to pollinate crocuses?

> When you see your Crocuses wide open in flower sally forth with a stick of sealing-wax or the amber mouthpiece of an old pipe in your hand . . . Rub whichever of the two unusual accompaniments of a garden stroll you have chosen, on your coat-sleeve if it be woollen, and hold the rubbed portion as soon as possible after ceasing rubbing near the anthers of an open Crocus, and you will find the electricity thereby generated will cause the pollen grains to fly up to the electrified object, and, what is more, to stick there, but so lightly that directly they are rubbed against the stigma of another Crocus they will leave the amber and be left where you, and Nature before you, intended them to be.

Rosalind Bliss

A hundred years after publication, Gussie's books are still extremely readable although, to get all the jokes, it helps to have a working knowledge of the Book of Common Prayer and the King James Bible. On the subject of the hardness of the New River water, for example, he wrote: 'Derived mainly from chalk wells, it is so hard that one feels it would be scarcely a miracle to walk on it . . .'

Although an immediate success, *My Garden in Spring* caused the wrong kind of stir when it came out, and for this Bowles had his friend Reginald Farrer to blame. Perhaps foolishly, he had asked Farrer to write the Preface, and the well-known rock-gardener, gardening writer and plant-hunter, famous for his overheated prose and odd ways, decided to use it as a none-too-subtle dig at Sir Frank Crisp, the rich, eccentric City lawyer who owned Friar Park, near Henley (later bought by George Harrison).

Sir Frank had built an enormous and lavish rock garden, which included a millstone grit replica of the Matterhorn, complete with alabaster top to resemble snow, and tin chamois peering from behind rocks. Farrer couldn't resist comparing this extravagance with Bowles's modest but high-quality rock garden, where plants flourished in semi-natural surroundings. Farrer didn't name names, but he didn't need to.

The Preface caused a tremendous hoo-hah, with Bowles being squarely blamed. Crisp's friend Miss Ellen Willmott, who gardened on an enormous scale at Warley Place, handed out to all and sundry at the Chelsea Flower Show a furious pamphlet, written by Crisp, that condemned Bowles. It was entitled 'MR E. A. BOWLES AND HIS GARDEN, A New Parable of the Pharisee and the Publican'. In it, Bowles was attacked for puffing up his own achievements in the Preface; Crisp, in his irritation, had failed to note its authorship. It says a great deal for Bowles that, beyond a gently reproachful letter to *Gardening Illustrated* after that periodical reproduced the pamphlet, he kept silent, neither publicly shifting the blame on to Farrer nor allowing his friendship with Farrer to be diminished by the latter's irresponsible behaviour.

My Garden in Summer was published later in 1914, while *My Garden in Autumn and Winter* came out the following year. Although very good, in my opinion they are not quite as appealing as *My Garden in Spring*, perhaps because Bowles's first love was always spring bulbs, especially tulips, irises, narcissi and crocuses. Farrer referred to him as '*crocorum rex imperator*' and indeed he was sought out for his knowledge of them all his life. He also wrote *A Handbook of Crocus and Colchicum for Gardeners* (1924) and *A Handbook of Narcissus* (1934) as well as many articles in the Journal of the Royal Horticultural Society.

No one appears to have had an unkind word to say about Bowles, and most people who met him found him excellent company. He was also extremely generous, both to his favoured charitable projects and with his plants. His great-great nephew, Brigadier Andrew Parker Bowles (the first husband of the Duchess of Cornwall), remembers being sent parcels of bulbs and plants by Bowles when he was away at school; and when I was serving my gardening apprenticeship in the 1970s, there were still people around who treasured plants in their gardens given to them by the man himself.

The best-known photograph of Bowles, taken in 1910, shows a man in a starched collar and tie, tweed suit and polished lace-ups, sitting on a garden bench, with one hand leaning on a garden fork, a wicker basket of garden tools and seed packets beside him, and a (presumably) faithful shaggy-haired terrier, called Kip, at his feet. He stares straight and benignly at the camera, the corners of his mouth lifting slightly in a diffident smile. It looks like the picture of just another perfect gent, living a respectable, privileged upper-class life at the turn of the last century. But the trilogy of books he wrote reveals somebody much rarer and more precious than that.

URSULA BUCHAN is a gardening writer who has recently given up the hurly-burly of journalism for the deep, deep peace of book writing.

Flashy but Irresistible

ANDREW NIXON

'Flashman is back,' declared the Labour leader Ed Miliband at Prime Minister's Questions on 11 May 2011. He was referring to David Cameron and he presumably meant to imply that the Tory was a boorish, ill-mannered bully, riding roughshod over the finer feelings of his Parliamentary colleagues. But I did wonder at the time just how well-chosen Miliband's 'insult' really was. Wouldn't any male politician be secretly *thrilled* to be likened to Harry Paget Flashman, the fictional Victorian soldier and adventurer?

True, Flashman is a bully, a liar, a coward and a cad – not qualities our leaders would normally want ascribed to them – but, damn it, he's a handsome fellow, square-jawed, walrus-whiskered, sword a-dangling beside a thrust-out pelvis encased in the finest breeches since Colin Firth made the ladies faint as Darcy. Wearing the self-satisfied grin of a man who's just spent the night with a grateful virgin or two . . . what man *wouldn't* want to be Flashman?

For here's another thing about Flashy: he's a quite phenomenal babe-magnet. In the pages of fiction only Don Juan and James Bond can match Flashman's prodigious sexual success. From prostitutes to princesses, Harry's had 'em all. He's rutted with Calcuttan dancing-girls and squired Native American squaws; been ravished by

George MacDonald Fraser, *Flashman* (1969), *Royal Flash* (1970), *Flash for Freedom* (1971), *Flashman at the Charge* (1973), *Flashman in the Great Game* (1975), *Flashman's Lady* (1977), *Flashman and the Redskins* (1982), *Flashman and the Dragon* (1985), *Flashman and the Mountain of Light* (1990), *Flashman and the Angel of the Lord* (1994), *Flashman and the Tiger* (1999), and *Flashman on the March* (2005) are all available from HarperCollins in paperback, each priced at £7.99.

Ranavalona I, the savage queen of Madagascar; seduced Lillie Langtry, the celebrated actress and mistress of Edward VII; and run through most of the *Kama Sutra* with Jind Kaur, the Maharani of Punjab. He once noted that his favourite lovers were Lakshmi Bai, Rani of Jhansi, the Chinese Dowager Empress Cixi, and Lola Montez, the latter 'a Queen, an Empress, and the foremost courtesan of her time'. Halfway through his life he counted up 478 conquests. He was married, too.

In fairness, perhaps Miliband was referring to the Flashman of *Tom Brown's Schooldays*, the insufferably preachy work by Thomas Hughes in which Flashman is chief tormentor of the 'fags' at Rugby School and a bully of the first order. Whatever the case, the fact is that the author George MacDonald Fraser adopted Hughes's Flashman, bestowed the forenames Harry and Paget upon him, gave him a lifespan (1822–1915) and sent him off to conquer the world of blood-and-thunder Victorian adventure fiction in an extraordinary series of cult novels. And it is this Flashman who will spring to mind among the vast majority of British voters for whom the name means anything at all.

In the first book in the series, *Flashman* (1969), Fraser purported to have 'discovered' Flashman's papers in an antique tea-chest in a Leicestershire saleroom, and he presented himself as their editor rather than their author. The faux-scholarly style, complete with extensive factual footnotes and appendices, and the references to genuine historical figures and events, convinced a number of reviewers in the USA (several of them academics) that *Flashman* was the real memoir of a soldier in the First Anglo-Afghan War.

Which is extraordinary, because Fraser's second masterstroke is that, though a risible coward wholly lacking in moral fibre, by a series of flukes, bluffs and coincidences, in every one of the twelve novels Flashman always ends up looking like a hero. By 'turning tail and lying and posturing and pinching other chaps' credit', he generally emerges with the girl, the swag and another medal for valour. Those

MAJOR-GENERAL HARRY PAGET
FLASHMAN, K.C.B. K.C.I.E.
1822–1915
After Lady Elizabeth Butler

Daniel Macklin

who see through his bluster and spot the craven rascal beneath have an unfortunate habit of popping their clogs before he can be exposed. Not that Flashman doesn't suffer along the way. Over the course of the series he becomes embroiled in virtually every military misadventure of the nineteenth century, including the Retreat from Kabul, the Charge of the Light Brigade, the Indian Mutiny and Custer's Last Stand.

Here I must admit that nearly everything I know about Victorian international affairs I've learned from the Flashman series. Given that they are ultimately a set of derring-do pastiches, this is an odd admission to make. But Fraser's attention to period detail and his ability to conjure up a place and a time rank him alongside the finest historical novelists. Since Flashman presents his own character at its very worst in these 'confessional' journals, we are inclined to believe him; and when his narrative wanders from verifiable historical fact Fraser 'corrects' him in the footnotes. Before reading *Flashman and the Dragon* (1985), for example, I had never known of the enormity of China's Taiping Rebellion. In it at least 20 million people died – more deaths than in the First World War that followed over five decades later.

Though they rattle along at a furious pace, Fraser's novels aren't for the squeamish. The setting of *Flash for Freedom* (1971), for example, is the African-American slave trade and the novel contains not only a stream of shocking scenes but also the highest incidence of the 'n-word' in any book I've ever read. In *Flashman and the Great Game* (1975), the horrors of the Siege of Cawnpore – an episode in the Indian Mutiny when 120 British women and children were massacred by sepoys and their hacked-up remains thrown into a well – are recounted in grisly detail. Fraser is utterly unsparing in his depiction of man's inhumanity to man; of our sad species at its basest.

This might suggest that George MacDonald Fraser was a misanthrope. He may well have been; certainly he believed that Britain had gone to the dogs by the 1970s and then got progressively worse. During the decades before his death in 2008 he lived on the Isle of Man (which only abolished the birching of petty criminals in 2000), from where he opposed the conversion to metric measurement and emitted, between Flashman novels, eye-watering tirades against political correctness. This is not to dismiss Fraser as a Colonel Blimp, nor to suggest that he shared the views of his whoring, racist, sexist literary creation. Rather, he was an idiosyncratic individual who loathed the stifling conformity of the liberal Left, which he saw as crushing personal freedom of thought and expression.

Fraser's own life was extraordinary enough. Born in Carlisle in 1925 to Scottish parents, he enlisted at the age of 18 in the Border

Regiment and served in Burma during the Second World War, an episode recounted in his remarkable memoir, *Quartered Safe Out Here* (see p.50). Later in life he found himself mingling with the Hollywood A-list, for he wrote a number of movie scripts, including those for *Octopussy* and *The Three Musketeers*.

But it was the Flashman series which established his fame, and which will surely ensure his immortality. For, as devotees of the series know, beneath the raw comedy and the thumping action, beneath the sex and violence and Flashy's appetite for devilment, there is another strand, one which becomes increasingly apparent through the series. Contrary to their reputation, there is a strong streak of moral rectitude in Fraser's books. Because his own persona is all bluff, Flashy is able to see through every set of Emperor's New Clothes he encounters. His evaluations of bureaucratic folly are as clear-eyed as any great parodist, and he doesn't have much time for armchair generals either. Consider this from *Flashman at the Charge* (1973), before the Light Brigade sets off on its doomed charge towards the Russian guns at Balaclava:

> I'll tell you something else, which military historians never realise: they call the Crimea a disaster, which it was, and a hideous botch-up by our staff and supply, which is also true, but what they don't know is that even with all these things in the balance against you, the difference between hellish catastrophe and brilliant success is sometimes no greater than the width of a sabre blade, but when all is over no one thinks of that. Win gloriously – and the clever dicks forget all about the rickety ambulances that never came, and the rations that were rotten, and the boots that didn't fit, and the generals who'd have been better employed hawking bedpans round the doors. Lose – and these are the only things they talk about.

There speaks the voice of a real soldier – here, we suspect, Flashman is Fraser. Flashy also has a decidedly no-nonsense view of historical theories. How's this for a succinct, iconoclastic summary of the causes of the American Civil War, from *Flashman and the Angel of the Lord* (1994)?

> As you know, it was slavery that drew the line and led to the war, but not quite in the way that you might think. It wasn't only a fine moral crusade . . . the fact is that America rubbed along with slavery comfortably enough while the country was still young . . . it was only when the free North and the slave South discovered that they had quite different views about what kind of country the USA ought to be that the trouble started. Each saw the future in its own image: the North wanted a free society of farms and factories devoted to money and Yankee 'know-how' and all the hot air in that ghastly Constitution, while the South dreamed, foolishly, of a massa paradise where they could make comfortable profits from inefficient cultivation, drinking juleps and lashing Sambo while the Yankees did what they dam' well pleased north of the 36° 30′ line.

For all his misdemeanours, Flashman is surrounded by figures who are far worse, from Ranavalona I to Otto von Bismarck. All Flashy wants to do is to save his own skin and bed a few birds; his antagonists tend to want to flay everyone alive, either from a misguided sense of duty or simply because they are psychopaths. Above all, Flashman detests idealistic or nationalistic baloney, the hope-and-glory huff-puffery that prompts military leaders to send droves of young men to useless suffering and death in the face of all common sense. Take this view of the American War of Independence, again from *Flashman and the Angel of the Lord*:

> Point out [to an American] that Canada and Australia managed their way to peaceful independence without any tomfool Declarations or Bunker Hills or Shilohs or Gettysburgs, and are every bit as much 'the land of the free' as Kentucky or Oregon

and all you'll get back is a great harangue about 'liberty and the pursuit of happiness', damn your Limey impudence . . . You might as well be listening to an intoxicated Frog.

It's understandable, to be sure: they have to live with their ancestors' folly and pretend it was all for the best, and that the monstrous collection of platitudes which they call a Constitution, which is worse than useless because it can be twisted to mean anything by crooked lawyers and grafting politicos, is the ultimate human wisdom. Well it ain't, and it wasn't worth one life, American or British, in the War of Independence, let alone the vile slaughter of . . . the Civil War.

Romantic it isn't, but it makes you think. Ed Miliband meant to demean the Prime Minister by comparing him to Flashman. Yet we might ask: what would the world be like if all leaders really *were* more like Flashman? What, in fact, would it be like if *everyone* was like Flashman? Certainly there'd be a lot more philandering and infidelity and running away in the world, but it would also be a far less bloody place. Flashman is a soldier wholly without idealistic fervour and warlike instincts; if he had his way there'd have been no disaster at Balaclava, no massacre at Cawnpore, no slaughter at Little Bighorn; instead, men would be left to get on with their drinking, gambling, lechery and whoring in peace.

ANDREW NIXON is editor of 'The Dabbler' culture blog: www.thedabbler.co.uk.

The Making of Flashman

PATRICK MERCER

I was brought up on a diet of George MacDonald Fraser's anti-hero Flashman as he roistered and rogered his way around the Empire, and I reread many of the books while serving in Northern Ireland. But it was only later that I found out why so many of the details in the books rang true. Fraser had himself experienced war in all its facets.

There seems to be a bottomless appetite for military literature, ranging from grand strategy to tank spotters' manuals, most of it concentrating on the heat of battle. But Fraser's wartime memoir, *Quartered Safe Out Here* (1992), is about ordinary men and how they cope with the breadth and depth of war. It's not showy, it's not sensational, it's just wonderfully, almost mesmerically, written.

The book follows the doings of a handful of men in the 9th Battalion, Border Regiment, during their fight against the Japanese in Burma, and the obscure title is deliberate. The phrase comes from Kipling's poem 'Gunga Din' and is redolent of Queen Victoria's troops and their tribal enemies, for throughout the book, Fraser emphasizes how dated were the weapons and tactics and how primitive was the fighting.

If you want a litany of blood-letting, glamour and glory, then this is not it. Here is a beautifully drawn but simple story of what infantrymen do on campaign – most of which involves tedium, tiredness and the turgid business of living with disease and discomfort.

George MacDonald Fraser, *Quartered Safe Out Here* (1992)
HarperCollins · Pb · 384pp · £6.99 · ISBN 9780007105939

Occasionally, the book strays into the brutal work of killing, but for the most part it's about the pleasure that an educated man gets from the company of his uncomplicated comrades.

The blend of rough-cut affection between the troops in Fraser's section wraps itself round you from the very start, as a sort of khaki family emerges, with Corporal 'Tich' Little at the head of a brood of ill-assorted siblings. I suspect Tich soldiered at Agincourt and I've seen him in Afghanistan recently, for Fraser describes the long-serving, hard-as-nails warrior upon whom the British Army has always depended. We're told what a tough, capable, uncompromising soldier Tich is, yet he's kind and, 'when least expected, as gentle as a nurse'. Among Tich's command are a couple of professional soldiers like Parker, who has been in 'one uniform or another since boyhood', but most are lads from Westmorland and Cumberland who have volunteered for their local regiment to fight the Axis powers in the same way that their fathers fought the Kaiser.

Even so, few of them expected to find themselves so very far from home and in such isolation as the jungles and swamps along the Sittang River. And this is where the economy of Fraser's descriptions scores so heavily. The loneliness of Private Grandarse, his dislocation from a Cumbrian farm and his bewilderment at the monsoon are perfectly expressed by the man saying forlornly 'grand growing weather, this' as the rain sluices down.

Then there's 'Nick' Nixon. I had someone like him in my platoon in Crossmaglen. Nick's the chronic pessimist, the man upon whom the rest of the world gangs up, the private soldier who knows how to run the campaign better than any general and who greets every plan of battle with the phrase 'You'll all get killed!' But he never does. Nick survives the war, probably because he's 'cool and wise and never ruffled'. And there's Wedge: there was a Wedge in my lot as well, always wondering why we got the shitty end of the stick and why he seemed to be on 'stag' – or sentry duty – for longer than any other man.

Private Steele turns into Fraser's closest mate after a rite of passage that I saw many times myself – the squaddie fight. A Carlisle man, Steele habitually baits the author by calling him 'Scotch'. Fraser tolerates this until one day Steele adds the word 'bastard', and then fists fly. When the fight is over, Little first makes them shake hands and then puts them on stag together, after which they are inseparable.

This family is at the core of Fraser's account, and the death of The Duke shows how much they depend on each other and how close they have become. The Duke could be one of Kipling's 'Gentleman-Rankers', for he is rumoured to be related to royalty, talks with a cut-glass accent and, while courteous and obedient to his NCOs, is capable of treating senior officers like the 'veriest trash'. After surviving a number of battles, The Duke is machine-gunned by mistake during the chaos of a night alarm just after a furious row with a man called Forster, who professes to hate The Duke's privileged background. Even so, Forster volunteers to lower The Duke's corpse into its grave.

The brutality of combat is wonderfully understated. In the *Flashman* books, Fraser often describes death – though he never overplays it – but when he writes about the use of swords and bayonets in Burma, there's a realism that suggests a deeper knowledge. So, after a particularly vicious fight, the Company Commander is seen to be just 'frowning' at his bayonet which is bent double having been pulled from a Japanese soldier. Similarly, an enemy whom Fraser has shot is dispatched by an officer 'slashing at his head with a kukri'. How might this be described in today's 'war porn', I wonder? Not as simply as this – and it's simple because this author doesn't revel in it or even regret it, it's just his job.

Above all, it is the frankness of Fraser's own experience of fighting that is so arresting. The first time he shoots someone he says, 'he gave a convulsive leap and I felt that jolt of delight – I'd hit the bastard!' How many others would dare to say that about what they felt? Fraser is not exulting in death, he's simply telling us how pleased he was to remove the threat of a man who was brandishing a sword and roaring a war cry and who clearly intended to butcher one of his mates.

The memoir also reflects the way in which attitudes have changed. Fraser makes the assumption, for instance, that the experience of fighting a war of national survival (as had his father's generation) left an indelible mark upon his friends that is almost impossible to understand today. He suggests that viewing his war through the telescope of values that haven't been tempered by death or suffering is almost pointless. So he believes it was necessary to drop the atomic bomb, despite the fact that it is now thought that Japan was almost ready to surrender anyway. But 'almost ready' is too long for Fraser; 'almost ready' might have involved the death of Nick, or Grandarse or Wedge, and alongside these men thousands of Japanese simply did not signify.

Above all I delight in Fraser's unabashed love for his Cumbrians, his joy in their jokes and his clear respect for their courage and grit. Nowhere is this more obvious than in his reproduction and explanation of their dialects. All this combines to create an exceptional book, not really a war book at all, more a saga of deep trust and honour, yet the best tale of soldiering that I know. It made me regret I wasn't there in Burma to share such things.

PATRICK MERCER served as an infantryman in Ulster and Bosnia, and was decorated four times, before becoming BBC Radio 4's *Today* programme's defence correspondent. He is now a writer and novelist and the MP for Newark.

A Tourist in Search of Home

DAVID BARNES

Perhaps it was the cover that first attracted me to the book. It showed a headless man in a suit and tie, with a vast hinterland of minor characters stretching out to the edges. Though I didn't know it at the time, this image captures perfectly the concerns of Kazuo Ishiguro's novel *The Unconsoled*. Ryder, its protagonist, is both no man and everyman; as the quintessential modern character, he is empty as we are all empty.

The Unconsoled was Ishiguro's big risk, the novel that divided critics, that John Carey and *The Times* called a 'masterpiece' but that other critics greeted with incomprehension. I came to it shortly after its publication. It was 1997 and I was 17, developing a taste for Kafka and for surreal and miserable Russian novels – the tortured faith of Dostoevsky, the angsty absurdism of Gogol's 'Diary of a Madman', 'The Nose' and 'The Greatcoat'. In those days, Central and Eastern European fiction seemed to speak to my adolescent self far more than the peaceful English classics. I would imagine the looming neo-Gothic quads of my boarding-school as a snowy Prague or Petersburg through which I would wander like one of Kafka's protagonists.

And, funnily enough, *The Unconsoled* reads a little as if it's been translated into English from Czech, Russian or Polish; the language seems strangely stilted. The writing projects a sense of comic unease. Compare its opening with that of Kafka's *The Castle:*

The taxi driver seemed embarrassed to find there was no one –

Kazuo Ishiguro, *The Unconsoled* (1995)
Faber · Pb · 544pp · £8.99 · ISBN 9780571225392

not even a clerk behind the reception desk – waiting to welcome me. He wandered across the deserted lobby, perhaps hoping to discover a staff member concealed behind one of the plants or armchairs. (*The Unconsoled*)

It was late in the evening when K arrived. The village was deep in snow. The Castle hill was hidden, veiled in mist and darkness, nor was there even a glimmer of light to show that a castle was there . . . Then he went on to find quarters for the night. The inn was still awake, and although the landlord could not provide a room and was upset by such a late and unexpected arrival, he was willing to let K sleep on a bag of straw in the parlour. (*The Castle*)

Both have the same mannered humour and dry delivery. The opening of Kafka's novel parodies the Nativity story, one from which – as a Jew in Catholic Prague – he may have felt excluded. There is 'no room at the inn' and K, the 'unexpected arrival', must sleep on the straw. In the Ishiguro, the humour is more surreal; when do hotel staff 'conceal' themselves behind potted plants? Both protagonists arrive to strange welcomes; the land surveyor in *The Castle* has been invited but, like Christ, is unwanted. By contrast Ryder, the international concert pianist in *The Unconsoled*, is expected but, as the novel proceeds, is unable to bear the burden of the demands placed upon him.

In both novels there are strange jumps in time and space, and absurd coincidences, in *The Unconsoled* often extremely funny. Frantic to escape from a claustrophobic party, Ryder walks into a broom cupboard. A man's leg is painfully amputated but turns out to have been prosthetic all along. The manager of the hotel Ryder is staying in drives him for hours to get to a reception in a building which turns out to adjoin the hotel's annexe, so that Ryder can simply walk home.

At other times the narrative leaves me disturbed and anxious. Ryder is escorted by a pack of newspaper reporters to have his photo taken in front of a controversial monument. All the time he can hear them calling him a 'difficult shit', yet he says nothing. A friend of Ryder's (who just happens, with various other acquaintances and possibly Ryder's own family, to be living in the city where he is performing) is banking on the fact that she knows the famous Ryder to impress her friends. But Ryder is unable to announce his presence in front of the friends, or even open his mouth, instead reddening and contorting in front of the mirror like a pig. His face, he tells us, 'had become bright red and squashed into pig-like features, while my fists, clenched at chest level, were quivering along with the whole of my torso'.

This weird humour is strangely infectious. When I shared a house in London a few years ago with a couple of fellow enthusiasts, we'd frequently revert to talking in a strange Ishiguro voice: 'Ah yes, that's sure to be most useful', 'You must convey my gratitude', 'I am heartened to discover' and so on. While some critics think Ishiguro's style is his weakness, to me *The Unconsoled* is a delightfully rich exploration of awkwardness and social unease.

As in Kafka, the humour and the creeping anxiety are not contradictory but belong together. The protagonists, like clowns, are denied their dignity; we can only laugh a despairing laugh. But while the book seems to parallel Kafka, it also feels like a parody of Kafka. The nameless labyrinthine city of *The Unconsoled*, a weird synthesis of central European culture, is not the Prague of K, but the Prague (or Vienna, or Krakow, or Berlin, or Vilnius) of globalized tourism.

And Ryder is the typical tourist, everywhere yet nowhere, wandering the Old Town trying to feel a connection to a history that is not his. Stability and rootedness elude him, and the book, like a lengthy session of psychoanalysis, returns again and again to the figures of Ryder's (possibly dead) parents, who remain just outside the narrative.

While Ryder is desperately trying to piece together the different parts of the strange jigsaw that is the city, at the same time it feels oddly familiar to him. He may have a wife and son living there; he may actually have lived there himself. But we're left feeling that the very same thing might happen in the next town he visits – that each new journey is a confrontation with his own past.

The book unfolds like one of those dreams in which we're lost in places that are both familiar and strange, where our wandering seems always tantalizingly about to end but never does. Ryder's quest is all our quests for identity, in an age when we fear all places are becoming the same, one in which we feel lost, even when we're at home.

For many of Ishiguro's protagonists – from the butler Stevens on his journey through England in *The Remains of the Day* to the displaced musicians in Venice in his short-story collection *Nocturnes* – home is an elusive concept. And then one remembers that behind the wandering musician Ryder is the Japanese-British musician and writer Ishiguro, whose perspective on the global mix of cultures and the figure of the traveller is both totally modern and uniquely his own.

DAVID BARNES regularly gets lost in the alleyways of cities like Prague, Venice and London. In his spare time he masquerades as an academic and has written on such diverse subjects as hip-hop lyrics, Victorian architecture and Italian fascism.

Neither a Borrower . . . ?

OLIVER PRITCHETT *on some more elementary do's and don'ts of book etiquette*

Every year the registrar of Public Lending Right issues a report on the authors whose books have been most often borrowed from libraries. You can be sure these days that Danielle Steel, Josephine Cox and James Patterson will be up there with the leaders, but it might be more interesting, I think, to discover the name of the author whose books we borrow most often from each other. We need more information about these delicate transactions between friends. I'd also like to know the title of the book which is most often borrowed and never returned, and I'd be disappointed to learn that it was something like *A Sensible Guide to Home Plumbing* or *The Grouter's Friend*.

There are so many mysteries. What is the longest time anyone has held on to a book before returning it? Was it handed down from generation to generation in one family or did it travel the world from friend to thief to cousin? I am also anxious to establish the identity of the person who, in 1974, lent me *The Aeronauts: A History of Ballooning, 1783–1903* by L. T. C. Rolt. It is still on my shelves waiting to be claimed.

I can't answer these questions, but I believe I can give some guidance on etiquette and tactics in this dangerous game in which it can be so easy to make an enemy for life by reducing a neighbour's set of Lawrence Durrell's *Alexandria Quartet* to a trio, or by leaving a chocolate stain on a friend's treasured copy of John Prescott's memoirs.

First we need to make a distinction between active borrowing and passive borrowing. You are a passive borrower when someone presses a book into your hands and insists that you really *must* read it. This may be a friend simply wishing to share a pleasure with you. Even so, rules apply. You can't hang on to the book for six months then return it saying: 'Actually, I thought it was rubbish.' Read quickly and enthuse.

As a passive borrower you may also encounter the power lender. This is someone who likes to control other people's reading habits and dishes out books to acquaintances as if he were distributing windfall apples to the humble peasantry. He harries you for your response. 'How are you getting on with Otto Verleiber's *Ruminations*?' he asks. 'I've got volumes two to five for you when you are ready.'

You are now trapped, doomed to Verleiber's ponderous pondering for months to come, and after that your power lender has already lined up André Prêteur's *Pensées* for you. The best thing is to refuse straight away, to say: 'I have made it a firm rule never to borrow a book. I'm sorry, but I have seen too many friendships destroyed . . .' Put on your Sydney Carton 'far-far-better-thing' expression and gaze into the middle distance. Your look of suffering may become more convincing as you realize that you have now talked yourself out of your regular supply of the works of Minette Walters, which you will have to borrow from another source, but at least you have kept your freedom.

Now a word of advice to active borrowers – sidle. Don't march up to your host's bookshelves and start making your selection. Admire the furnishings in the room first, comment on the charming view, pat the family dog. It's a good idea, if possible, to do a recce first, so that you can appear to come across your chosen volume by chance. 'Ah,' you say, as if taken by surprise, '*The Mayor of Casterbridge*. Is it any good?'

Never borrow a book from its author. Only a rotter would do such a thing. Go and buy it. It is dangerous to borrow a book which someone else has borrowed from a library. Who is going to pay the fine when it is overdue? As a rough general rule, a work of fiction should be returned to its owner within three weeks. For non-fiction, there is a little more leeway; add a week for a chunky biography. Anything by

Jamie Oliver or Nigella Lawson should be back with its owner, unsmeared, within a week.

I am often asked if it can ever be acceptable to borrow a book and then lend it to a third party. I have known this to be used as a strategy in matchmaking when the object is to introduce the book's owner to the third party as a possible mate. The third party eventually returns the book directly to its owner and a relationship blossoms through a shared love of, say, Edith Wharton. The danger is, of course, that it all ends in tears and resentment and a dog-eared copy of *The House of Mirth*. Then you will be blamed.

Incidentally, if you are a young lady and you own all 48 volumes of Walter Scott's *Waverley* novels and a gentleman of your acquaintance sets about borrowing them, one by one, it might be worth considering the possibility that his intention is to woo you very slowly and methodically. If you like the idea but wish to speed him up, try to get him interested in a novella.

For the lender, the greatest concern must be to get his or her book returned in good condition and in good time. One approach, by the writer and hostess Dorothy Nevill, who died in 1913, was to put a sticker inside each volume saying 'This book was stolen from Lady Dorothy Nevill'. Flann O'Brien once said page 96 was 'the secret page on which I write my name to catch out borrowers and booksharks'.

A bossy lender will record the deed in an imposing ledger or demand a deposit, but will then get a reputation for meanness. You may stick in handsome personalized *Ex Libris* bookplates, all beautifully engraved and perhaps slyly pretending to be your family's coat of arms, but your shelves will be stripped bare as soon as word gets round the community of avid and unscrupulous collectors of bookplates.

As I have shown earlier, borrowing a book should be an art. Similarly, there is a good bad way and a good way to *return* the borrowed book. Obviously, it's bad form to leave jottings in the margin (unless you are incredibly famous) and it's not a good idea to leave a bookmark revealing the fact that you gave up at page 39. Toffee papers between pages are not recommended. When you return a book you must make it clear that doing so has been inconvenient. If possible, wait for a day when there is deep snow to trudge through or, at the very least, wind and driving rain. As you approach the lender's house it's a good idea to limp. Arrive in the early morning or late at night, saying, 'I wanted to return this wonderful book to you the *minute* I had finished it.' Then you can linger and discuss the plot, prose style and characterization. At length.

It is also advisable carelessly to leave some kind of present inside the returned book, as a gesture of gratitude. A £5 note would be vulgar and insulting, but an old gas bill (preferably a final demand) would be acceptable, or a detailed credit card statement. Other people's bills are always fun. Best of all, you could leave an indiscreet letter from a mutual friend. The lender then will be really keen to let you borrow many more volumes, in the hope of receiving further instalments.

Like the lender of a fiver, the lender of a book is often unfairly resented simply for wanting to get back what is his – or hers. Lenders are forced to talk their way into other people's houses to check on the bookshelves – and even the bedside tables – to see if they can track down some much-missed novel. All they get is accusations of snooping.

There is one possible answer. When you lend a book, go to the borrower *the very next day* and ask if you can have use of their bicycle for a week or so. Or their cafetière or perhaps two of their dining-chairs or maybe their au pair. How can they refuse? And when they get itchy and want their property (or their au pair) back, they know what they have to do.

The last payment OLIVER PRITCHETT received from Public Lending Right was £1.33 in 2004.

Dreamwork

KATHRYN PEAK

When my sister was 10 she bought a rather battered copy of a book called *Marianne Dreams* at our school summer fair. A few years later, when she decided it was too young for her, she handed it on to me. I love puzzles – not particularly the kind that have to be solved, like crosswords, but ones that intrigue in the same way as a complex painting or a spider's web. *Marianne Dreams,* published in 1958, is that kind of novel. Its plot is driven by mysterious connections – invisible threads that join together people and things in worlds both real and imaginary – and while the story may be resolved at the end of the book, the puzzle remains.

Although its author Catherine Storr (1913–2001) did write fiction for adults, it is for *Marianne Dreams* that she is best known, and for *Clever Polly and the Stupid Wolf,* written for younger children. Her most successful stories were based on those she told her own children when they were growing up, or stories devised with her children or their friends as characters. *Marianne Dreams* tells the story of a girl who is able to manipulate her dreams through the pictures she draws. The events in her dreams, dramatic and fraught with difficulties, become as real and as important to her as the world she inhabits when awake.

I was 9 when I first read the novel. By that age I was a voracious reader and took a book to bed with me each night. I would read a

Catherine Storr, *Marianne Dreams* (1958)
Faber · Pb · 192pp · £5.99 · ISBN 9780571202126
Marianne and Mark (1960) is out of print.

chapter – or two if I could get away with it – before my mother insisted on lights out. This worked well until I read *Marianne Dreams*. Though it is aimed at children of around 8, I can't imagine children of 11 or 12 not being at least a little disconcerted by it. I was scared but completely hooked, and went to sleep each night with disturbing images in my head, inevitably followed by nightmares.

The Marianne of the title is a girl convalescing after a serious illness, which keeps her bored and bedridden for many weeks. When she finds a good drawing pencil she uses it to draw a house with a front path and a fence, and long grass as far as the eye can see. She also draws large rocks beyond the fence. Soon afterwards she falls asleep and dreams of the house. But in this dreamland of wind running through the open prairie, she feels compelled to enter the house to get away from something outside.

There are no birds or animals or people on the prairie, just the wind and the grass and a niggling feeling that something is very wrong. This sense of aloneness is compelling. In most children's stories, even in moments of danger and fear there is usually some comfort to be drawn from friends or surroundings, to make the journey easier. The world that Marianne dreams of is bleak. The landscape is empty and forbidding, and the house is old, empty and unfurnished, as if it might be haunted.

When she is awake, Marianne adds things to her picture. She draws a boy sitting in one of the upstairs windows, and when she dreams again she meets Mark, who is also an invalid. Indeed, the two children realize that in the waking world they have the same peripatetic governess to help them with their schoolwork. This connection between them, a tenuous one in the real world, a solid one in the dream world, remains a mysterious piece of magic in the story that is deliciously never explained.

The two children do not immediately become friends. Their fears and insecurities make them at first despondent and grumpy with one another. In a moment of malice Marianne blackens out Mark's window, raises the height of the fence to make it prison-like, adds more rocks, and on each rock draws a single eye.

The unease that pervades the novel becomes more tangible when the children discover that the rocks are watching them. Then slowly, imperceptibly, the rocks start to move inside the fence and approach the house. The children must find a way to escape from the house and garden and the oppressive nightmare that Marianne's picture has created. It is this escape that takes up the remainder of the novel and ultimately provides a resolution.

Catherine Storr was well aware that her book was frightening. 'We should show [children] that evil is something they already know about or half know,' she once wrote. The novel was written during a period in the Fifties and early Sixties when she was practising as a psychiatrist in London, having qualified as a doctor in the 1940s. She had always wanted to be a writer, having studied English at Cambridge with this in mind. By retraining in medicine she hoped, among other things, that she 'would get that experience of life which was wanted in my writing', and one can see in the psychological nuances of the book her clinical knowledge being put to use.

She did go on to write a sequel, *Marianne and Mark*, which was published in 1960. However, it is a fairly straightforward story in which Marianne finally meets Mark in the real world when they are both teenagers, and it contains little of the atmosphere and intensity of its predecessor. *Marianne Dreams* also spawned several spin-offs. It was made into a children's television series in 1972 and into a film called *Paperhouse* in 1988, and Catherine herself wrote the libretto for the operatic adaptation which was first performed in 2004.

Rereading *Marianne Dreams* now I can see that it foreshadows much that I have gone on to read and write as an adult: stories that play with the threads that connect people, that shift between worlds and question what is real. Catherine loved writing for children for this very reason, because she believed that children 'make this move between the practical and the imaginative with no difficulty at all . . .

because they can hold both concepts in their minds at once, without the one spoiling the other'.

My copy of *Marianne Dreams* is now very battered indeed. It no longer has the power to give me nightmares, but I still hold it in great affection, and have never quite outgrown it. Catherine Storr once wrote that it is difficult to specify a body of work that can be called 'children's literature'. Instead, she said, we should 'consider the books themselves which, whether written for children or not, children want to read.' The same could be said of fiction for adults, depending, I suppose, on how much we can still see the child within us, whose world view we may not have quite given up.

KATHRYN PEAK has had far too many jobs for her age. She is currently on maternity leave, using available time (when her daughter naps) to redraft her new novel. She is very grateful to her daughter for napping long enough for this article to be written.

A Plug for Dr Brewer

A. F. HARROLD

Imagine if you will that the Internet has broken down, that your browser's no longer working, your modem lights up but doesn't connect, that, in fact, the whole world-spanning web has simply vanished, ceased to be, been switched off, that your computer has been reduced in a moment to nothing more than a winking typewriter with the bonus of Photoshop and Solitaire. That great, vast and glowing source of information, misinformation, mail-order shopping and friendly gossip has shut up shop and left you sitting at your desk twiddling your thumbs. Crikey. Well, as inhuman as such an event may appear, it is actually very similar to how the world was before, say, the turn of the century.

It's sobering to realize, for me at least and I'm sure for many readers, how quickly I have adapted and subsumed this other realm into normal life. How when I'm sitting at my desk here, working on a poem or a novel, and a query comes to mind, my first impulse is to slip a search into Google or Wikipedia and have an answer delivered to me without moving from my seat, and in mere moments, as quick as that (and to those who argue the Internet is full of lies, well, the answer is to be selective about what you believe and where you read it). Not only does this seem normal, it seems almost indispensable.

But when I lift my eyes from my desk I see that my flat is filled with beautiful untidily stacked bookshelves, and my lintels, sills and tables wobble with papery piles, because although the Internet can

Brewer's Dictionary of Phrase and Fable (1870: 18th edition, 2009)
Chambers · Pb · 1,488pp · £15.99 · ISBN 9780550100306

beat a reference book for speed and efficacy, still nothing beats a book for pleasure.

Several sorts of pleasure immediately come to mind: first of course, the aesthetic: the look, the weight, the feel, the smell of the thing; and then the browsing joy of letting a book flop open where it will, of flipping a page forward or back, of riffling through and stopping as and when and wherever. Although the web lets you follow tangents and links hither and thither, just like following the keywords through a reference book, and although Wikipedia has a 'random entry' button that dips you in, as it says, at random, the serendipitous thrill of opening an encyclopaedia and letting your eyes fall and follow where they will is something awfully special.

Back in the mid-nineteenth century, when there was no Internet, when news took weeks to travel from country to country and even then could barely be trusted, books finally came into their own. Dr Ebenezer Cobham Brewer began his publishing career by writing educational books and the weekly penny magazine *Popular Educator* in the 1840s for the burgeoning number of adult autodidacts, and then, later, elementary textbooks for schools.

It was while compiling these books (*A Guide to Science, A Guide to Roman History* and *My First Book of Bible History/Geography/ Reading and Spelling/English History* etc. etc.) that the Doctor caught the first glimmer of the idea which would make his name known for a century:

> The popularity of these books brought me in a large number of questions on all imaginary matters. I kept these questions and their answers till they grew into a large book, when I sorted them and made the nucleus of the *Dictionary of Phrase and Fable.*

Dr Brewer's *Dictionary* (1870) is a uniquely curious lucky dip of a book – part anthology of proverbs, part almanac, part Classical dictionary, part trivia. The man in the street who hadn't the advantage of schooling in Latin and Greek could now delve to his heart's content, learning snatches of stories, myths and legends, of history and folklore. The breadth of the book, of one man's labour, is still impressive.

Unremarkably it is the only book of his forty or so still to be in print and continuously so 140 years later (although I like the sound of the *Appendix to Dr Brewer's Guide to Science, to which is added Poisons and Accidents, the antidotes and remedies* (1859), which has a nicely *Under Milk Wood* ring to it); and even though the contents have been continually updated (he revised the second edition himself in 1895), it remains a treasure trove of language and human history that sits in a place not quite occupied by any other reference work. Many overlap his, but Brewer's sits at a nexus.

Dipping almost at random and following links back and forth to other pages, today I learn that Cockney is a Middle English word meaning 'cock's egg' which was 'applied to the small malformed egg occasionally laid by young hens; hence applied to a foolish or spoilt child, or a simpleton'. Later the word came to be applied 'by country folk, the majority of the population, to townsfolk generally for their reputed ignorance of country life, customs and habits'. Its specific attribution to certain Londoners came about in the seventeenth century.

Following that I read a little history of the Bow Bells: one given in 1472 by John Dun to be rung at 9 o'clock at night 'to direct travellers on the road to town', and a bigger one given by William Copland in 1520 'for the purpose of "sounding the retreat from work"'.

Just under that is the phrase 'Bow-window in Front' which means 'a big belly' (the same as a bay-window). I have a bit of one myself, but never has it been so delightfully described.

Just under Bay-window is Bayard, which was the name of a horse that Charlemagne gave 'to the four

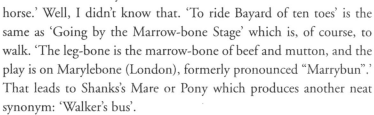

sons of Aymon. If only one of the sons mounted, the horse was of ordinary size; but if all four mounted, his body became elongated to the requisite length . . . The name is used for any valuable or wonderful horse.' Well, I didn't know that. 'To ride Bayard of ten toes' is the same as 'Going by the Marrow-bone Stage' which is, of course, to walk. 'The leg-bone is the marrow-bone of beef and mutton, and the play is on Marylebone (London), formerly pronounced "Marrybun".' That leads to Shanks's Mare or Pony which produces another neat synonym: 'Walker's bus'.

Opposite that is Shallal – 'In former days in Cornwall, a band of rough music which visited newly-married couples and those suspected of immorality'. Which entry leads us to Skimmington, a more specific piece of rough music:

> To make an example of nagging wives by forming a ludicrous procession through the village accompanied by rough music to ridicule the offender. A man, mounted on a horse with a distaff in his hand, rode behind the woman with his face to the horse's tail, while the woman beat him about the jowls with a ladle. As the procession passed a house where the woman was paramount the participants gave the threshold a sweep. The event was called *riding the Skimmington.*

And there are references to descriptions in Samuel Butler and Walter Scott, and a reminder that 'the *skimmity ride* causes the death of Lucetta Farfrae' in *The Mayor of Casterbridge*.

Next I learn that 'By the skin of one's teeth' comes from the book of *Job* and that 'To skin a flint' ('to be very exacting in making a bargain') is not only the origin of the noun skinflint, but also has a Latin antecedent, *lana caprina* (goat's wool), which means 'something as worthless as the skin of a flint or the fleece of an eggshell'.

A little further down the page is 'To skylark about': 'To amuse oneself in a frolicsome way, jump around and be merry, indulge in mild horseplay. The phrase was originally nautical and referred to the sports of the boys among the rigging after work was done.' We're all well aware of the nautical nature of many of our turns of phrase, but that's one I just learnt.

But Brewer isn't just a languorous meander. There are also lists, brilliant useful useless lists, a quiz-setter's delight: Tricolour (a list of countries and their tricoloured flags); The Wise (people (kings) given that surname); Popes numbered among the saints; Rings noted in Fable and Legend; Dying Sayings ('many of these are either apocryphal or have survived in inaccurate versions'); Giants of the Bible; Giants of Legend and Literature; Giants of Other Note; Misers; and Famous Libraries, for example.

Two final entries I spotted while flicking through just now: 'Runcible Hat, Spoon – In Edward Lear's "How Pleasant to Know Mr Lear" there is mention of a runcible hat and in "The Owl and the Pussycat" a runcible spoon. What *runcible* denotes is not apparent. Some who profess to know describe the spoon as a kind of fork having three broad prongs, one of which has a sharp cutting edge.' (There is no entry for 'spork'.) And Dickens. To play the dickens (also 'What the dickens?'): 'To play the devil. *Dickens* here is probably a euphemism for the devil or Old Nick, and is nothing to do with Charles Dickens.' That last has, to my ear, the air of a man laying an urban myth to bed with a 'and that's the last time I'll say it'.

I hope this little jaunt round Dr Brewer's dictionary has given a taste of what's in it. It's like a fine Sunday walk up on the Downs or a rambling conversation with an old friend: that is to say, it's familiar in a warm way, may not teach you anything you didn't know, but might remind you of some things you'd forgotten. When you open it up, you don't know exactly which way you're going to go, which turning you might take this afternoon or where you might end up.

There's probably nothing in there you couldn't find on the Internet easily enough, but the fact that Dr Brewer sat in his little office upstairs at Cassell's in the late 1860s thinking, 'What else should I put in?' and writing it all down, I think deserves recognition. And his book has at the very least one important thing which means it wins out over the inexhaustible library of the Internet, and that is that it works perfectly well even in a power cut.

A. F. HARROLD is an English poet and performer who can often be seen on the stages of cabaret and comedy clubs and at literary festivals doing things that aren't quite normal. Somehow he manages to get by: www.afharrold.co.uk. The illustrations in this article are by B. Lodge.

Dream of Old England

ANDREW SINCLAIR

When I was but a boy and a bit in the last World War, I had a dream. I walked down Polstead Road in Oxford to Aristotle Lane. And I stopped off by the canal with my fishing-rod before going over the shuddering railway bridge on to the vast expanse of Port Meadow with its snapping swans. 'Break your leg, they can,' I was told. 'With one chop of their beak.'

I tried to catch tiddlers, the dace and the roach, and put them in a jam-jar, though they were too muddy to eat. Sometimes a shire horse would plod up the canal path. It towed on a rope a dark barge, yet bright with painted colours, on its way to Tartary or beyond. Or so I supposed. Steering the craft, a heavy man with a cloth cap. I took out my rod as it passed. In those days and nights of rations and the black-out, I wanted him to call out to me, 'Ahoy, boy. Come aboard. And shiver me timbers.' But he never did.

A picture in our little house and a book excited me. There was a coloured print of Sir Walter Raleigh in Elizabethan hose and doublet, sword and feathered hat, explaining his faraway adventures to two children on a beach. And there was the magic of Kipling's *Puck of Pook's Hill*, where the young brother and sister act *A Midsummer Night's Dream* and meet the pixie Puck, who tells them of the people of the Hills of Old England, imps and trolls and brownies and goblins, who live by Oak, Ash and Thorn. And he relates the history of Ancient Britain in fairy story and fact.

Rudyard Kipling, *Puck of Pook's Hill* (1906)
Dover · Pb · 288pp · $9.95 · ISBN 9780486451473

H. R. Millar

At 8 years old, I could not tell what from which. For my sense of wonder had not left me, even in the shrapnel of war. When not watching the sparks climb in tiny fireworks on the soot at the back of the grate above the glowing coal, I read *Puck of Pook's Hill*. And from the chapters on 'Weland's Sword' and 'The Knights of the Joyous Venture', so much of my future work would unconsciously come. As Puck implied, the spell of Merlin could last a lifetime.

The tales the pixie told to Kipling's children were entrancing. And there were verses, too. Puck called himself 'the Oldest Thing in England, very much at your service – if you care to have anything to do with me'. And I did care. Country reality I found in old Hobden the hedger, who was descended from charcoal-burners. His son was a Bee Boy, not quite right in the head, but he could pick up swarms of bees in his naked hands, and take the honey from their combs.

The Sword forged by Weland, smith of the gods and kin to Thor, was dark grey and wavy-lined and inscribed with runes. That weapon fell into the hands of the Norman knight Sir Richard, who fought at the battle of Hastings, where the Saxon King Harold was killed. Later, I would try to transcribe those strange signs along with the Ogham script, but then I read of the prophecies on the Sword:

> A Smith makes me
> To betray my Man
> In my first fight.
> To gather Gold
> At the world's end

I am sent . . .
It is not given
For goods or gear
But for The Thing.

How marvellous and mysterious! And Sir Richard is captured by a raiding Danish ship and transported to Africa to trade beads for gold. There he fights Devils, or actually gorillas, before he returns home. Now his place is taken by Parnesius, a Centurion of the Thirtieth Legion, sent to guard the Great Wall of the North. There he struggles against the Picts, led by Allo, who was tattooed blue, green and red from his forehead to his ankles.

The Wall is attacked by the Winged Hats, Norse raiders in search of booty. They are like wolves, for they come when they are not expected. The would-be Roman Emperor Maximus withdraws most of the legion to fight in Gaul, but Parnesius hangs on with his few resources, until he is relieved.

Next come 'Hal o' the Draft', an early scribe with a small ivory knife carved as a fish, and Master John Collins who makes the serpentines, the old ship's cannon, for English pirates, who build churches with their loot. And then Tom Shoesmith enters from Romney Marsh, where the folk have been 'smugglers since time everlastin''. There lives the Widow Whitgift, a Seeker and a prophetess and a wonderful weather-tender, who loses a blind son and a dumb son to become ferrymen. The tale ends with the smugglers' caution:

Them that asks no questions isn't told a lie.
Watch the wall, my darling, while the Gentlemen go by!

Finally, I found out what happened to the African gold, as the runes on the Sword had forecast. The Jewish physician Kadmiel was to promise a bribe to King John to sign Magna Carta for English liberty, before sinking the rest of the hoard. As was inscribed on the wavy blade:

The Gold I gather
Comes into England
Out of deep Water
Like a shining Fish
Then it descends
Into deep Water.

What a prophecy of the rise and plunge of the British Empire across the Seven Seas! And written by a man who was said to be an imperialist. To me, Kipling is rather more a mythmaker. While many have wondered at his understanding of India and its mysticism in *Kim* and his other tales of the Raj, his grasp of Celtic folklore has been forgotten. Yet outside Andrew Lang's fairy tales, *Puck of Pook's Hill* remains the most concise and evocative recall of the legends of Britain.

Later I was to collect all of Kipling's works in the Twenties' Macmillan editions, bound in red leatherette and stamped with gold. My *Puck of Pook's Hill* has on its outer cover an elephant's head, clutching in its trunk a lotus petal below the sign of the swastika, the ancient Indian emblem of well-being. The illustrations are by the admirable H. R. Millar in the style of the romantic realism of the time, sketching a line of truth into a web of past fable.

Another mythmaker had been a neighbour in my Oxford childhood. T. E. Lawrence was said to have written some of *The Seven Pillars of Wisdom* in the garden shed next door. When my brother or I hit a cricket ball over the wall and broke a window of that place which had conjured up Arabia, we did not know our sacrilege and got into trouble. But there you are. Who could believe that Polstead Road had also housed a hero of the First World War, the conflict in which Kipling had lost his son and turned to spiritualism to seek him again?

When I wrote my novel *Gog* about the myths of Albion, I tramped over the Lothian hills from Edinburgh to York Minster in seven days with only £1 in my pocket. And sleeping on Hadrian's Wall as the

Roman sentries had, I found myself reciting the anthem of Kipling's centurions:

> Mithras, God of the Morning, our trumpets waken the Wall!
> 'Rome is above the Nations, but Thou art over all!'
> Now as the names are answered, and the guards are marched away,
> Mithras, also a soldier, give us strength for the day.

I had learned the lines as a wartime schoolboy from *The Dragon Book of Verse.*

When I visited the Orkneys and Greenland, Nova Scotia and Rhode Island, while following the voyages of the Vikings in their search for gold in America, my subsequent book *The Sword and the Grail* lurched in the wake of Kipling's account of Weland's Sword and the Winged Hats on their African adventures. It is not so much that the child is father to the man. More certain is that the books read by a child are the mother of its imagination.

ANDREW SINCLAIR has always tried to do things beyond his powers. All unreached, except for one good film and three good books. Coasting into old age, he still wonders what is to come.

Lytton's Characteristic Specimen

ARIANE BANKES

Rereading 'The End of General Gordon', the fourth of Lytton Strachey's portraits in *Eminent Victorians* (1918), is an awful reminder of our failure to learn from history. Gordon's and Gladstone's ill-fated machinations in the Sudan are so redolent of Britain's recent misadventures in Afghanistan and Iraq as almost to take one's breath away: substitute either country for Khartoum, and you have an example fearsome enough to deter any but the most fatuous sabrerattler from going near the place, let alone attempting to influence its political fate from thousands of miles away.

Yet it was the recent past, not the future, that preoccupied Strachey when, in the run up to the First World War, he squirrelled himself away in a cottage near Marlborough to compose this and its companion essays on Cardinal Manning, Florence Nightingale and Thomas Arnold. Honesty being the byword of the Bloomsberries, he decided to re-evaluate with an untarnished gaze the gilded reputations of these *éminences grises* from the recent past, all of them prominent members of a British Establishment whose collective failings had brought the country to its knees in the supremely pointless conflict that raged about him as he wrote.

And this he set about with relish. The mighty were delicately dislodged from their pinnacles, cut down to size by the waspish wit and gleeful scrutiny of this most laconic member of the Bloomsbury set. His companion Dora Carrington's best-known portrait depicts him

Lytton Strachey, *Eminent Victorians* (1918)
Penguin · Pb · 288pp · £8.99 · ISBN 9780140183504

lying under a coverlet, his foxy ginger beard spread neatly before him, his long and delicate fingers clasping a book, his eyes behind owlish spectacles utterly absorbed in its contents. From this languorous and pensive figure would come a volume that would upend and overturn all decorous assumptions of biography to date, a volume to set tongues wagging, reputations spinning and tills ringing. For *Eminent Victorians* proved a wild success on publication and went into multiple editions straight away.

Lytton Strachey, drawing by Dora Carrington

Given his iconoclastic approach, Strachey was rather miffed to get mainly enthusiastic reviews; he had expected to stir up a storm of controversy, but, he confessed to Lady Ottoline Morrell, 'the reviewers are so extraordinarily gushing that I think something must be wrong'. It was with some relief that he read a broadside from Edmund Gosse in the *TLS* and carping reviews from other critics, concerned at his lack of historical method, which indeed he would not have got away with today: he eschewed all notes and used only secondary sources, embroidering freely on these when he felt the story might benefit from some imagined aside or other.

But then his methods fitted the objectives that he laid out with such brio in his Preface. Claiming that too much was already known about the Victorian age for it to be truly understood, he suggested it was not by 'the direct method of scrupulous narration' that the historian would unlock the past, but by a 'subtler strategy'.

> He will attack his subject in unexpected places; he will fall upon the flank, or the rear . . . He will row out over that great ocean of material, and lower down into it, here and there, a little bucket, which will bring up into the light of day some characteristic specimen, from those far depths, to be examined with a careful curiosity.

Pity his 'characteristic specimens' – one would probably not want to be examined by Lytton Strachey with 'careful curiosity' if one had the choice. On the other hand, he was intensely interested in human nature, believing that 'Human beings are too important to be treated as mere symptoms of the past,' and these examinations made for marvellously entertaining and instructive essays that illuminate as clearly the motives and manners of his subjects as the times in which they served – for they all did serve, in true Victorian style, some greater good, whether it be Empire, Queen or God.

God, it must be said, was one of the sticking-points. As an avowed non-believer, Strachey deplored the pseudo-Christianity that underpinned Europe's war and that provoked the Bishop of London to claim in 1915, 'This is the greatest fight ever made for the Christian religion.' Humbug and hypocrisy were the twin targets on which Strachey skewered the Machiavellian Cardinal Manning, shadowing his sinuous climb up the greasy pole of nineteenth-century Evangelism to become a leading intellectual light of the Victorian age.

Sticklers might well have accused Strachey of flippancy for comments such as the following, on the demise of the Oxford Movement: 'The University breathed such a sigh of relief as usually follows the difficult expulsion of a hard piece of matter from a living organism, and actually began to attend to education.' But the majority of readers relished his wit, while his frank dissection of Manning's ambitious manoeuvrings and dastardly campaign to unseat his erstwhile mentor Cardinal Newman – last seen sobbing in defeat and despair over a garden gate – made for compelling reading.

Florence Nightingale, the saintly 'Lady of the Lamp', had a slightly easier time of it. Due credit was given to her extraordinary transformation of the infernal hospitals at Scutari, a task normal mortals would hesitate even to contemplate, but Strachey goes on to dissect her peculiar brand of double-edged heroism: certainly not 'that simple sort so dear to the readers of novels and the compilers of hagiologies . . . it was made of sterner stuff'. He continues, 'Beneath her cool and calm demeanour lurked fierce and passionate fires,' and her complete mastery of officialdom he could only put down to 'the fixed determination of an indomitable will'.

Back in England, half-dead from exhaustion (indeed she was to remain half-dead for the rest of her long life), her will became, if anything, more indomitable, and from her sick-bed she continued to be the scourge of the military hospital establishment, of government and indeed of all the powers that be. Woe to her opponents, such as the unfortunate Lord Panmure at the War Office (known as 'The Bison') who stood 'four square and menacing, in the doorway of reform' – the wily Miss Nightingale discovered his Achilles heel, and soon made swift work of him.

But her supporters and friends deserve even more sympathy: the faithful Sidney Herbert was driven to an early grave by her impossible demands, and her devoted disciple Dr Sutherland, who once had the temerity to take a holiday, was swiftly recalled and 'did not repeat the experiment'. The adage 'No man is a hero to his valet' comes to mind here, although Strachey does concede that through her tireless bullying she managed to move administrative mountains, and that her obsessive, indeed neurotic need to subdue others to her will eventually gave way to a more conciliatory stance, if only at the cost of going soft in the head.

Strachey's most pointed barbs are aimed at Thomas Arnold, the famous headmaster of Rugby School. Perhaps memories of his own unhappy schooldays intensified his criticism – 'At school I used to weep – oh! for very definite things – bitter unkindness and vile brutality,' he once wrote to Leonard Woolf. His portrait of Arnold is of a man one would draw lots not to sit next to at dinner: pious, pompous, self-righteously severe and nursing a horror of 'what St Paul calls revelling' – and with short legs, to boot. Arnold's ambition 'to make the school a place of really Christian education' left little room in the curriculum for fact or observation; he would much rather his charges believed that the sun went round the earth than skimp on 'Christian and moral and political philosophy'. So much for Darwin and the new science of evolution, so much for spirited and timely debate. Arnold's sermons were legendary and awe-inducing, and were collected in five large volumes among his many other works of scholarship, for like Florence Nightingale he could not tolerate a moment's idleness and was forever expatiating on learned subjects that he had recently mastered, Sanskrit and the Slavonic languages among them.

Credit where credit is due, however – the public-school system was in a state of virtual anarchy before Arnold's arrival at Rugby; Eton was a human bear-pit presided over by the ineffectual Mr Keate, whose only remedy for everything was to flog his boys until they wept. Arnold's fervent belief in higher things did bring his school within the bounds of civilization, and by sheer force of character his fame spread far and wide. He made schooling respectable, he introduced the prefectorial system and put games on a par with godliness, but Strachey's contention is that he funked true liberal educational reform. He certainly left England's public schools in that strange limbo between the old order and the new, places where arcane traditions lived on still, and where generations of boys wept into their pillows by night while being inducted into the dubious values of superannuated belief systems by day.

Which brings me back full-circle to General Gordon, and specifically his End. How did a man so clever, so shrewd, so experienced in the paths of imperial politics (in the Sudan as much as China and elsewhere) end up marooned in the backwater of Khartoum, besieged by thousands of enraged followers of his opponent the Mahdi, to the point where all was lost? According to Strachey, the problem lay in Gordon's obsessive religiosity – this was a man who read almost nothing but the Bible, over and over again – allied to manic self-belief; when bent to the service of colonial hubris, and in particular to the implacable will of that gimlet-eyed statesman Gladstone, who proved his nemesis, Gordon's fate was sealed.

Eminent Victorians has been credited with reforming the genre of biography, but while it broke the mould it did not chart wholly new ground: Boswell had, after all, written a refreshingly unvarnished life of Dr Johnson, and John Aubrey had invented the 'brief life' over a hundred years before that. A fashion for fervent obsequies and reverent tomes had then become fashionable, however, and in taking a considered swipe at those four grandees of a grandiloquent age (it was to have been eight, but he ran out of steam), Strachey was also undermining the whole edifice that had supported (and, in Gordon's case, destroyed) them. In doing so he ushered in a new era, of more transparent values, of less cant and humbug, of deft selection and interpretation rather than dogged regurgitation of fact. Brevity, he claimed, was the first duty of the biographer; his second was 'to maintain his own freedom of spirit'. If only 'life writing' would more faithfully observe the first – but there is no shortage of the second these days, and for that at least we must be grateful.

ARIANE BANKES edits *Canvas*, the Friends' magazine of the Charleston Trust, when not running some festival or other.

Chips Triumphant

JOHN HAMMOND

On my bookshelves are several well-thumbed copies of *Good-bye Mr Chips*. One is a first edition with a delightful jacket illustration by Bip Pares of Mr Chips asleep in an armchair. Another is a film 'tie-in' paperback showing Peter O'Toole and Petula Clark in a scene from the 1969 musical version. A third is a beautifully bound special edition signed by the author and the artist H. M. Brock. And yet another is of Robert Donat and Greer Garson in a scene from the classic film version made in 1939.

Why do I have so many copies of the same book? Simply because it is one I frequently reread and it pleases me to read it in a variety of editions. *Good-bye Mr Chips* is a novel one can revisit again and again without tiring of it – surely one of the acid tests of a work of literature. Now firmly established as a twentieth-century classic, its origins are interesting.

One day in November 1933 a little-known writer named James Hilton was invited by the *British Weekly* to write a 3,000-word short story for publication in their Christmas issue. For this he would be paid £50, a considerable sum in those days. Hilton was then living a precarious existence as a freelance journalist and he badly needed the money. The only snag was that the story had to be written within a fortnight; otherwise it would be too late for the Christmas number.

Throughout the first of his precious two weeks he had a classic case of 'writer's block'. He racked his brains to think of an idea but

James Hilton, *Good-bye Mr Chips* (1934)
Coronet · Pb · 128pp · £7.99 · ISBN 9780340043592

inspiration simply would not come. At last he decided to go for a bicycle ride to clear his brain. He set off towards Epping Forest (he was then living with his parents at nearby Woodford Green) and happened to pass some ancient school buildings covered in Virginia creeper. As he looked at the old school an idea suddenly bobbed up in his mind and he saw the whole story in a flash. He pedalled home at furious speed and sat down at his typewriter to hammer out *Good-bye Mr Chips* in four days. He wrote later:

> I am chary of using the word 'inspiration', which is too often something non-existent that a writer waits for when he is lazy; but, as a matter of record, *Good-bye Mr Chips* was written more quickly, more easily, and with fewer subsequent alterations than anything I had ever written before, or have written since.

The publishers were delighted with the story but surprised to find that the 3,000 words they had requested had now become 18,000 – the length of a short novel. Nevertheless they sensed that this was something special and decided to publish it in its entirety in their Christmas supplement. A few months later the *Atlantic Monthly* in America followed suit.

The story is an affectionate portrait of the life and career of Mr Chipping (known to generations of staff and pupils as 'Chips'), a schoolmaster at Brookfield, a boys' boarding school. He joins the staff in 1870 at the age of 22 and remains there until he retires in 1913 at 65. During the First World War he is recalled from retirement and becomes Acting Head for a brief period, finally stepping down in 1918. He dies in 1933, a popular and respected figure who has become a Brookfield institution.

Good-bye Mr Chips gives a bird's eye view of his long career as he looks back on his years as a Classics master – his arrival at Brookfield as a young and diffident teacher, his slow gaining of confidence, his triumphant marriage to the vivacious and forward-looking Katherine Bridges, her death in childbirth two years later, his popularity with boys and staff as a kindly and wise teacher, his rich sense of humour, the mingled nostalgia and happiness with which he surveys his long years as a school-master, the sweeping social changes he has witnessed with the passing of the Victorian age and the coming of the twentieth cen-tury. With the unfolding of the years he has become almost a revered figure, 'the guest of honour at Old Brookfieldian dinners, the court of appeal in all matters affecting Brookfield history and traditions'. Through it all shines the personality of 'Chips', a quiet and gentle man, modest about his achievements but not afraid to express his opinions on matters of principle.

Chips is no dry-as-dust pedant. He expresses himself forcibly on educational matters, as when a new headmaster deprecates Chips's 'old-fashioned' methods:

> These examinations and certificates and so on – what did they matter? And all this efficiency and up to dateness – what did that matter, either? . . . No sense of proportion. And it was a sense of proportion, above all things, that Brookfield ought to teach.

In holding these views Chips is flying in the face of the prevailing orthodoxy of his time, and even today many would question the notion that the teaching of values is as important as the teaching of the curriculum.

Chips goes out of his way to ensure that his pupils respect the views of others. At the time of the Boer War for example he points out that the Boers are engaged in a struggle bearing a marked simi-larity to that of some English heroes; during a railway strike he is pointedly on good terms with a striker; at the height of anti-German feeling during the war he deliberately announces that a former

German master has been killed while fighting on the Western Front. Chips stands for tolerance, compassion and understanding in an age when hatred and mistrust are widespread.

Hilton based the character of Mr Chips on a number of schoolmasters he had known in real life including his own father, John Hilton, who taught in Walthamstow, London, for many years. His principal source, however, was W. H. Balgarnie, senior Classics master at The Leys School, Cambridge, where Hilton was a pupil from 1915 to 1918. Years later Hilton confided to the headmaster: 'Balgarnie was, I suppose, the chief model for my story, so far as I had one; certainly in my school life his was a personality I have never forgotten.' In modelling Mr Chips, Hilton took from Balgarnie his shrewdness, his infectious humour, his love of verbal jokes and his strong sense of discipline. Balgarnie too loved to reminisce about the school and liked to keep in touch with former pupils.

Good-bye Mr Chips was published in book form in 1934, sold 130,000 copies within the first ten months and has been in print ever since. Perhaps the finest tribute among a plethora of favourable reviews on publication was paid by the novelist Howard Spring:

> Here is triumphant proof that a little book can be a great book. Mr Chips deserves a place in the gallery of English characters. Never have I known more beautifully rendered a man at perfect peace with life, a finer setting forth of what happy dreams may come when you are old and grey and full of sleep.

The novel has also been filmed four times, most notably in the 1939 version starring Robert Donat, adapted as a stage play, dramatized for radio and translated into twenty languages, including a Japanese version translated by Professor Kiyoshi Ikeda, a former pupil of The Leys School. Fittingly too, the name 'Chips' has come to be synonymous with a venerable schoolmaster who commands the respect of both staff and pupils and can look back on a long and distinguished career.

It would not be an exaggeration to say that it was *Good-bye Mr Chips* that launched James Hilton on a highly successful literary career. His most famous novel, *Lost Horizon*, was actually published before *Chips* but its initial sales were disappointing. It was the phenomenal success of *Good-bye Mr Chips* which led to an increasing interest in Hilton and to reprints of his earlier works. He had at last 'arrived' as a fully fledged author.

Not long after he was invited to Hollywood and became a scriptwriter, working on classic films such as *Mrs Miniver* and *Madame Curie*, and advising on adaptations of his own novels. Those four days he had spent typing away in a white heat of enthusiasm proved in the end to be the decisive turning-point of his life.

JOHN HAMMOND has written on Wells, Poe, Orwell, Stevenson and Defoe. He is also the founder of the James Hilton Society: www.jameshiltonsociety.co.uk.

The illustrations in this article are by Bip Pares and appeared in the original 1934 edition of *Good-bye Mr Chips*.

All They Had Was Hank

COLIN DUNNE

Try it yourself. Assemble a handful of chaps of pensionable age –
because these will be men whose voices were wavering between treble
and tenor in the 1950s – and ask them if they remember the name
Hank Janson. I guarantee you an interesting reaction – first the joy
of slowly dawning recognition, then a shifty flush of guilt as they
realize why they remember it so well. During the Fifties Hank Janson
was by far the most famous writer of sexy books in Britain. These
days, young men have sex education. Then, ten years after the war,
we had Hank.

If I may remind you of that distant time. There were no bare
breasts in the tabloids, no contraceptive pill for either the day before
or the morning after, no half-naked ladettes writhing on the pave-
ments of an evening, no sex lessons featuring courgettes, almost no
single mums. Our television chef, a plump little chap with a beard
called Philip Harben, never used the f-word but quite often the g-
words: gosh and golly. A cry of 'Get them out for the lads' would
have meant nothing to anyone. Hard to imagine, but it's true. With
so little information, it's a miracle the human race didn't die out. As
I say, all we had was Hank, which is probably why, six decades later,
his name is still remembered with mingled pleasure and shame.

I thought I was the only one who remembered him until I came
across his name in Simon Gray's diaries. 'The titles alone drove my

---

Telos Publishing have reissued 12 of Hank Janson's novels, with Reginald
Heade's original cover artwork, in paperback at £9.99, along with Steve
Holland's *The Trials of Hank Janson*, also in paperback at £12.99.

blood wild – *Torment for Trixy* – *Hotsy, You'll Be Chilled*,' he wrote. Gray had a secret library of Jansons: he ripped off the lurid covers before squirrelling the books away in his bedroom, often under loose floorboards. When he discovered at the age of 65 that there was a whole website devoted to Hank and his works, he was quite beside himself: 'I really went through the most astonishing tumble of emotions, the confusion of desire and thrilled shame.'

Now I wouldn't for a moment suggest that reading Hank helped the late Simon Gray become one of our most distinguished playwrights, but if his memory was imperishable for the two of us, how many others still dreamed of *Torment for Trixy?*

When confronted with a dilemma of this nature, I rely on the Petersfield Golf Club test. If you do not already know this, the Petersfield seniors are respectable retirees, men whose BMWs bear a shine to match that of their polished brogues: they pay their taxes, prune their privets and seldom do anything to frighten the horses. I asked a dozen of them if they remembered the name. They all did, with one exception.

'Aha, you must be referring to the author of those racy crime thrillers,' said Peter. ''They were well-thumbed and passed from one adolescent to another.'

Clive's response was even more accurate: 'Pulp-fiction writer who specialized in potboiler thrillers featuring lurid sexual exploits (very anodyne by today's standards).'

John pointed out that they were not books you wished your mum to find you reading and Des recalled that they were sold in brown paper wrappers – 'hence the brown paper carpet in my bedroom'.

If Simon Gray and the grandees of the Petersfield Golf Club can cherish these memories, I feel a little less self-conscious about my own. At Ermysted's Grammar School in the Yorkshire Dales, on the rare occasions when we got our grubby paws on a Hank Janson, we fell upon it like wolves. For younger readers, I must point out that our entire sex education consisted of the sports master, Mr Swainson, giving a mumbled and red-faced account of the reproductive system of the frog. (This could account for the fact that many of my schoolmates were strangely drawn to women with long legs, bulging eyes and cold skin. Luckily, they were not in short supply in Yorkshire.)

However, that was all the information we had to go on. A few hundred yards up the road, the pupils at Skipton Girls' High School could have helped out but seemed unwilling to do so.

If you were to walk up the Ermysted school drive now, turn left under the arch into the third-form block, immediately right into the cloakroom, then fish behind the huge old iron radiator in the corner, you might well find *Skirts Bring Me Sorrow*, which I left there in 1954. I seem to remember someone's older brother had bought it from a

B. Lodge

stall in Bradford market. We kept it rolled up behind the radiator and, between double physics and Latin, four or five of us – with one on sentry duty – would retrieve it and read out the rude bits.

I have it here before me. Not the original, of course, but a reissue by the small publisher Telos, who have reprinted a range of Hank's books. The cover prices it at 1s. 6d, describes Hank as 'Britain's bestselling American author', and bears an illustration of a long-legged redhead wearing a silk rag held in place only by her remarkable thoracic development.

It was illustrations such as this, together with the tough-guy titles, that made the books so irresistible. Nothing in our previous reading – 'Wilson the Wonderman' in the *Wizard* comic and Red Circle school adventures in *Hotspur* – had prepared us for *When Dames Get Tough, Sweetheart, Here's Your Grave* and – my personal favourite –

Slay-Ride for Cutie. Each had a cover showing a half-naked woman, sometimes chained or roped, and usually staring in some fear at something unspeakable about to happen just outside the frame. As we huddled over *Skirts Bring Me Sorrow* in the cloakroom, we rather thought she might be looking out for our headmaster, M. L. Forster, who was a deft hand with the bamboo cane himself.

So who was Hank? His cover biography makes Ernest Hemingway sound like a bookworm. Born in England, stowed away on a fishing trawler, dived for pearls in the Pacific, spent two years whaling in the Arctic, worked all over America as a truck-driver, news reporter and private detective. Served in Burma during the war. Returned to England where he spends his time gardening and writing in Surrey. It sounds almost as if someone had made it up. Someone had. Hank, as it happens. This was one of his better pieces of fiction, to fit the image his readers wanted.

The truth is less picaresque. Stephen Daniel Frances – his real name – was born and brought up in grim poverty in South London. Fiercely left-wing, during the First World War he was a conscientious objector. Later, after producing a few articles, he founded a small publishing company and began writing his tough, sexy thrillers. He took the name Hank because it rhymed with Yank, although Stephen Frances himself never set foot in America. As far as readers were concerned, Hank Janson was the author and, as crime reporter for the *Chicago Chronicle*, the hero. Frances almost seemed to believe his own publicity. In his rare interviews, he appeared as Janson with a hat and a mask.

The books just rolled out: *Lady, Mind that Corpse – Smart Girls Don't Talk – Baby Don't Dare Squeal – Don't Mourn Me Toots*. And they sold in their millions. Every six weeks a new story about fillies and frails and broads ran off the press, 100,000 copies of each for his readers, waiting clammy-handed.

Even that wasn't enough. When Stephen Frances tired of being Hank Janson he would become Ace Capelli, Johnny Grec or Duke

Linton. At one time he was producing a book a week, nearly 300 altogether, with sales of over 13 million in the Forties and Fifties. While one book was being typed for the printer, he was already well into the next one; sometimes five titles were being printed simultaneously. 'I felt more like a factory than an author,' he said. A profitable factory though. He drove a Daimler and bought a home in Spain, where he died in 1989.

He liked to claim that he had vicars and doctors among his readers, and no doubt he did. But most of his books, I suspect, would have been found in Army camps and factories, not to mention behind my school radiator and beneath Simon Gray's floorboards.

Hank started publishing in 1948 but didn't hit trouble until the end of paper rationing in the 1950s produced a flood of magazines and books, and Britain was able to indulge in one of its periodic attacks of Puritanism. The police began raiding bookshops and newsagents, seizing and destroying thousands of 'obscene' books and prosecuting booksellers. His distributor went to jail.

Hank had a near miss. Asked if he was the writer of these obscene books, he denied it. It was the truth. As he pointed out later, he didn't write them, he dictated them. His publishers went into liquidation, booksellers and newsagents were reluctant to stock him, and no one wanted to defend poor old Hank.

But then the tide turned. When the same obscenity laws were used against serious books, there were letters to *The Times* and voices raised in Parliament. Steve Holland, author of *The Trials of Hank Janson* (also republished by Telos), says: 'Few writers can be said to have had such an impact on literature. Without Janson, we might still be reading expurgated versions of *Lady Chatterley's Lover*, and *Fanny Hill* might be consigned to history.'

I can't say that influencing the course of English literature was at the forefront of my mind as we crowded over our copy in the cloakroom, and I doubt if Simon Gray's thoughts went in that direction either. Steve Holland says the books were real page-turners and were written with a breathless energy that makes them very readable. So sixty years on, I picked up *Skirts Bring Me Sorrow* to see if I could find what it was that held me, most of Ermysted's third-form, Simon Gray and half the members of the Petersfield Golf Club in thrall all those years ago.

And there it all was: 'magic shudders of pleasure . . . a dame who'd been starved of love . . . the fragrance of her bare shoulder . . . deliciously quivering beneath my hot hands . . . her mouth was moist and hungry .' – the book was deliciously quivering in my hot hands. Now I remembered what it was we found in Hank Janson. There was no information about sex, none whatsoever. What he showed us was the wicked excitement and danger of sex. That was something you couldn't get from tadpoles and for that alone we owe him something.

And did it deprave and corrupt us? Oh, I expect so. You only have to look at the Petersfield Golf Club seniors to see that.

COLIN DUNNE has published eight novels and written articles and columns for everyone from the *Mirror* to *The Times*. His career as a writer, a story marked for the most part by cruel humiliation and bitter disappointment, is recorded in his latest book, *Man Bites Talking Dog*.

Bibliography

E. A. Bowles, *My Garden in Spring*   38

Brewer's Dictionary of Phrase and Fable   66

Richard Cobb, *The French and Their Revolution; Paris and Elsewhere*   21

George MacDonald Fraser, *Flashman; Royal Flash; Flash for Freedom;*
Flashman at the Charge; Flashman in the Great Game; Flashman's Lady;
Flashman and the Redskins; Flashman and the Dragon; Flashman and
the Mountain of Light; Flashman and the Angel of the Lord; Flashman
and the Tiger; Flashman on the March   43

—— *Quartered Safe Out Here*   50

James Hilton, *Good-bye Mr Chips*   83

Kazuo Ishiguro, *The Unconsoled*   54

Hank Janson, the novels of   88

Rudyard Kipling, *Puck of Pook's Hill*   72

Philip Larkin, *Collected Poems*   29

John Masefield, *Grace before Ploughing*   7

John Cowper Powys, *Wolf Solent; A Glastonbury Romance; Weymouth*
Sands; Maiden Castle; Porius; Autobiography; Petrushka and the Dancer   33

Terry Pratchett, *Small Gods*   15

Suzanne St Albans, *Mango and Mimosa*   11

Catherine Storr, *Marianne Dreams; Marianne and Mark*   62

Lytton Strachey, *Eminent Victorians*   77

The *Slightly Foxed* Crossword No. 3: Answers

Across: 1 STOPPARD; 5 SPEARS; 9 MADELINE; 10 TAYLOR; 12 ENOBARBUS;
13 CHIME; 14 TROY; 16 EREWHON; 19 EMERSON; 21 GOTH; 24 STRAW;
25 COLERIDGE; 27 ADMIRE; 28 GILLIGAN; 29 SANCHO; 30 EGREMONT
Down: 1 SAMUEL; 2 ODDJOB; 3 POLKA; 4 RENT BOY; 6 PRATCHETT; 7 ALL
RIGHT; 8 SERGEANT; 11 ESME; 15 RUSHWORTH; 17 LESSWAYS; 18 DERRIMAN;
20 NICK; 21 GOLDING; 22 ADAGIO; 23 PEANUT; 26 ROLFE

Coming attractions . . .

LINDA LEATHERBARROW revisits the country girls

MICHELE HANSON meets a confederacy of dunces

RALPH HARRINGTON remembers the Bird Man of Singapore

CAROLINE CHAPMAN appreciates a legacy

CHRISTOPHER RUSH flees the madding crowd

HILARY SPURLING lingers with the afternoon men

JUSTIN MAROZZI discovers some lost oases

ANTHONY GARDNER plays tennis with the Masai

 The Royal Society
of **Literature**

5th March: Karen Armstrong, 'What Is Religion?'
Venue: Kings Place, 90 York Way, London, N1 9AG
Book via www.kingsplace.co.uk (020 7520 1490)

19th March: Richard Davenport-Hines and Frances Wilson
on the *Titanic*

23rd April: Susannah Clapp, Caryl Phillips and Bidisha,
'A Celebration of the Work of Angela Carter'

The RSL hosts regular talks, discussions and readings. Fellows and Members are invited to attend any of these meetings. Members of the public are also welcome to attend. There are up to 30 tickets for non-members at each event, which are sold on the door on a first-come-first-served basis from 6 p.m. for £8 (£5 concessions). All meetings begin punctually at 7 p.m., and are held in the Kenneth Clark Lecture Theatre, Courtauld Institute of Art, Somerset House, Strand, WC2, unless otherwise stated. For booking information visit www.rslit.org, call 020 7845 4677 or e-mail hazel@rslit.org. Membership of the RSL is open to all. Please call us on 020 7845 4676 or visit our website for further information.

A year's subscription to

THE REAL READER'S QUARTERLY

Slightly Foxed

If you have friends or family who you think might enjoy *Slightly Foxed*, why not buy them an annual subscription? We will send them a card with your greetings in their first issue.

Annual subscription rates
UK £36 Europe £44 Rest of the World £48

SLIGHTLY FOXED LIMITED
67 Dickinson Court, 15 Brewhouse Yard, London ECIV 4JX
tel 020 7549 2121/2111 · fax 0870 1991245
email all@foxedquarterly.com

STERLING CHEQUE · VISA · MASTERCARD

www.foxedquarterly.com
with secure online ordering facilities